The
Word
of His
Grace

The Word of His Grace

A guide to teaching and preaching from Acts

Chris Green

ivp Inter-Varsity Press

INTER-VARSITY PRESS

38 De Montfort Street, Leicester LE1 7GP, England

Email: ivp@uccf.org.uk

Website: www.ivpbooks.com

British Library Cataloguing in Publication Data

A catalogue record for this book is available from the British Library.

ISBN–13:   978–1–84474–075–7
ISBN–10:   1–84474–075–7

Set in Monotype Dante 10.5/13pt

Typeset in Great Britain by Servis Filmsetting Ltd, Manchester
Printed and bound in Great Britain by MPG Books Ltd,
Bodmin, Cornwall

Inter-Varsity Press is the publishing division of the Universities and Colleges Christian Fellowship (formerly the Inter-Varsity Fellowship), a student movement linking Christian Unions in universities and colleges throughout Great Britain, and a member movement of the International Fellowship of Evangelical Students. For more information about local and national activities write to UCCF, 38 De Montfort Street, Leicester LE1 7GP, email us at email@uccf.org.uk, or visit the UCCF website at www.uccf.org.uk.

Contents

Part IV: Living Acts

Preface

Studying Acts while being a pastor is a challenging exercise, because the comparison between the two realities is a humbling one, and as a leader one is in a position of responsibility. So I want to thank the two churches where most of this material was first grappled with – Christ Church, Bromley, and Emmanuel, Tolworth – for their tremendous support and encouragement as we sought, tentatively, to apply the lessons which emerged. They first heard the sermons included here, as well as many others which emerged from the underlying thinking.

Studying Acts while being responsible for training other pastors is even more humbling, because the comparison is even more shocking. The mistakes I make as a pastor are limited to one congregation, but the mistakes I make as a trainer are multiplied in churches all over the place. So I want to thank the thoughtful and helpfully critical members of the Cornhill Training Course who heard many lectures from me on Acts, and who cheerfully chiselled through to a clearer understanding of the text.

Churches are good places to learn as we teach, and so are theological colleges. My colleagues at Oak Hill have stimulated many thoughts, particularly Professor David Peterson and Dr. Matthew Sleeman, who are both engaged in serious academic research on Acts and who have nudged me in all sorts of ways. The College and the Kingham Hill Trust have also been generous in providing me with study leave to complete the project, and other members of the faculty have been either willingly taking on some of my responsibilities to free me up, or slowing me down with entertaining and caffeine-driven conversation. Thank you.

And to Sharon I can only say: what a privilege it is to be together, and to have been engaged in teaching Acts to the young children in church, including our boys Edward and Alex, even while I was finishing this book. Thank you too, and this is for you, with my love.

Chris Green
Oak Hill College, August 2004

1 | Introduction

Acts is a great book! It describes the most exciting phase in the history of the church, with wonderful pioneering work being done by courageous men and women, under the direct inspiration and guidance of the Holy Spirit. Miracles and healing combine with powerful preaching and an intensity of relationships that makes us think that we would love to be in such a church. Thinking more soberly, we realize that the miracles were often accompanied by martyrdom and the preaching, although powerful, was not always persuasive. But, that aside, there are a freshness and vitality running through Acts that make it a favourite book for churches to study together as they long to be the kind of people God wants them to be.

There is, of course, a downside: many or most (or even all) of our churches are nothing like the church we read about in Acts. The life and growth, passionate prayers and obvious love for Jesus do not seem to be the reality of what happens week by week. That wistfulness is fuelled by books reporting what God is apparently doing elsewhere in the world in ways that sound very similar to Acts – or at least the successful parts of it – and the gnawing feeling grows of guilt and doubts. Pastors, leaders and preachers wonder why the congregations they serve are not up to the Acts standard. Church members wonder why their leaders do not match the Acts standard. Acts seems to set the bar for vitality impossibly high and leaves us feeling disappointment with what God has provided.

Which is not what God intended. Acts does contain stories of intense excitement, it is true, but it also shows us church members who lie to their leaders; leaders who have major rows with each other; unfair legal processes; murder; persecution; and death. It would be a mistake to see the story of Acts, heroic and successful as it is, as one of unchallenged heroism and unbroken success. We should also be clear that the reason for the success lies not in the heroism, but in the promises of God. He is the one who plans and guides the route the gospel takes from Jerusalem to the ends of the earth, and if Acts has a hero at all, it is God.

So Acts is a great book for churches to study together, because it will encourage us to be passionate about God and his gospel and also realistic about the nature of the task we face. But Acts is also a long book, and that creates a problem for getting to grips with it. Not only that; because commentaries on books tend to be longer than the books they comment on, many commentaries on Acts are quite lengthy works. Because they are also committed to getting the details of the text right, it is very easy to become lost in a forest of detail.

This book is designed to be different and to supplement the normal kinds of commentaries. From the outset, in Part I, it takes the big picture of Acts and tries to make sense of it theologically, as a whole: a coherent and purposefully written narrative. From there it moves into Part II, which looks at the book in smaller sections as Luke seems to have arranged them, although all of these smaller sections are themselves several chapters long. But, just as walkers take out a compass to orient a map properly to the North Pole (the big picture) so that they can make sense of paths and villages (the small picture), so this guide is designed to orient each smaller part first of all within the larger picture. Then comes the time to ask the small-detail questions for which the normal commentaries are needed.

Because it is designed for those who preach or teach and who want guidance in communicating the relevance of Acts, the third section of the book contains some sample sermons. I have added these tentatively, because I am not holding them up as ideals to attain or as gold standards. Rather, they are examples of how the process of under-standing the big picture first – what I have called here the *architecture* of Acts – turns into a normal Sunday sermon.

You will need a good modern translation: the NIV is the one used throughout this book because of its widespread use. You will also need time. To read Acts attentively takes a couple of hours at least; to understand it properly, it needs to be read a number of times through, prayerfully and with pencil in hand. There is no substitute for that extensive, first-hand encounter with the book. Start working and enjoy this wonderful part of Scripture. As Paul said, it contains 'the word of his grace, which can build you up and give you an inher-itance among all those who are sanctified' (20:32).

Part I: Reading Acts

2 | Reading Acts

Acts is about as long as a single-volume book in the ancient world could be, which in today's terms is about the length and shape of a roll of kitchen paper. Luke's Gospel is about the same length again, and when taken together they make Luke the largest single contributor to the New Testament. But, where the Gospel narrative is familiar, Acts is much less well known, at least beyond the first few chapters. Even people familiar with the story find that Paul's missionary journeys merge into one another, the speeches overlap; the various hearings and trials before Felix and Festus lose their precise role; and the rationale for a whole chapter being given over to a shipwreck is difficult to see.

One reason is that, like much of the Old Testament, Acts is written as an extended story, or series of stories, with multiple characters and plot lines. When it comes to 1 or 2 Samuel, we do not think our confusion matters that much. But when it comes to Acts we do think that it matters, because it is more obviously our book. It is in Acts that God gives the Holy Spirit, and Christians are first called Christians. It is here that we see the first churches planted and the first evangelistic moves made. So this is our dilemma: we are passionately committed to the idea that the book matters, but we do not really know how to make sense of it.

But if we can discover some principles that will help to get a handle on a lengthy book like this, the pay-off will be enormous. Not only will we be able to make sense of Acts, we will be well on the road to making sense of 1 or 2 Samuel too – and Acts itself teaches us that they are books which point to Jesus (Acts 13:22).

Reading biblical narrative is a skill that can be learned, like any other, and there are various principles that can help in grasping the overall pattern of material. Taken together, they help to position each part of the book in Luke's intended purposes. There are many others that could usefully be added to the list, but the eight described can easily and helpfully be illustrated from within Acts.

Eight principles for reading and teaching from Acts

1. Look for the author's stated purpose
Luke makes it easier for us by stating from the outset what he intends to do.

> In my former book, Theophilus, I wrote about all that Jesus began to do and to teach until the day he was taken up to heaven, after giving instructions through the Holy Spirit to the apostles he had chosen.
>
> (1:1–2)

So, obviously, we expect a continuation of Luke's story of Jesus, in that what he *began* he will now continue. To put it starkly, Luke claims to be writing not the Acts of the Apostles, nor even the Acts of the Holy Spirit, but volume two of the Acts of Jesus.

So Luke's *first* stated purpose drives us back to the opening of his Gospel, where he writes an extended introduction to his work. He tells us of his careful research, of people and on paper, so that his reader, the same 'most excellent Theophilus', 'may know the certainty of the things you have been taught'.[1] We should expect Acts,

---

1. Luke 1:4

then, to function in the same way. It will reinforce the gospel to us and show how the historic claims about Jesus and his church are plausible. It is an open debate whether Theophilus was an actual person or a hypothetical 'Dear Reader' figure, because the name means something like 'Someone who loves God'. It is also unnecessary to debate whether this person was a Christian or not, because not only will the gospel be presented sufficiently clearly that a non-Christian may grasp it and understand it, but Luke will also show us serious and profound implications of it, that Christians today still spend a lifetime thinking through. His goal throughout this two-volume work, then, is *certainty* over the gospel, and we should bear that in mind as we read.

Luke's *second* stated purpose comes a few verses later, in 1:8. Jesus said,

> You will receive power when the Holy Spirit comes on you; and you will be my witnesses in Jerusalem, and in all Judea and Samaria, and to the ends of the earth.

This verse gives a fourfold pattern to the book. We shall expect first the giving of power; secondly, scenes in Jerusalem associated with being witnesses, with an explanation of what it means to be a witness and what they claim to have witnessed; thirdly, a move beyond the city to the surrounding land; and finally, a move to the ends of the earth. It is not difficult to see that simply as a fourfold scheme for the book: the giving of power (roughly, chapters 1 and 2), Jerusalem (3 – 7), Judea and Samaria (8 and 9) and the ends of the earth (10 to the end).

These markers are not just geographical; they tell a theological story too. Jerusalem was the City of David, and presumably that is why Peter makes so much of the relationship between David and Jesus in his Pentecost sermon. One of the major elements of this part of Acts is the motif of fulfilment. It is studded with Old Testament quotations and allusions in a way that is quite unusual, compared with the rest of the book. Judea and Samaria are not two randomly chosen areas, but the two halves of King Solomon's kingdom that were ripped apart by civil war under his son Rehoboam. Never again one nation, frequently at war, driven into separate exiles, the two rivals were promised a future unity in the new kingdom of God.

Only in Acts, as the news of God's new king, Jesus, is proclaimed in 'Judea and Samaria', is the promise fulfilled. The final segment, 'the ends of the earth', is also an Old Testament phrase with a promise attached. As Psalm 98:1–3 puts it:

> Sing to the LORD a new song,
>   for he has done marvellous things;
> his right hand and his holy arm
>   have worked salvation for him.
> The LORD has made his salvation known
>   and revealed his righteousness to the nations.
> He has remembered his love
>   and his faithfulness to the house of Israel;
> all the ends of the earth have seen
>   the salvation of our God.

There was a clear, repeated expectation that God would bless Israel in such a way that all humanity would be blessed, and that the blessing would explicitly involve salvation for the Gentiles. Jesus equally explicitly commands his followers that they are to implement this next phase of God's saving plan.

This gives a second purpose to Acts. It is to inform us, and excite us, and challenge us in the area of evangelism. Clearly there is a sense of completion at the end of the book, where Paul has arrived at last in Rome, and a case can be made for saying that the capital of the empire represents, in some sense, the ends of the earth. But, significant as Paul's arrival in Rome was, he consistently looked beyond it to further mission fields.

This is clear in Luke's *third* stated purpose, which comes at the close, in 28:30–31:

> For two whole years Paul stayed there [Rome] in his own rented house and welcomed all who came to see him. Boldly and without hindrance he preached the kingdom of God and taught about the Lord Jesus Christ.

The conclusion of a narrative is as important as its opening, and here Luke gives us further clues as to why he is writing. He is making it abundantly clear that he is not writing a biography of Paul or Peter.

Both of them have abrupt endings: Paul's is here, and Peter completely disappears from centre stage after his crucial speech in Acts 15:7–11. He is never mentioned again. This is only one of a number of such similarities between the two men to which Luke draws the reader's attention, as we shall see, but it is worth noting here, when it might otherwise look as if Luke did not finish his story. Luke intentionally removes his two principal human characters out of the spotlight so that the focus should lie elsewhere.

For what Paul did in Rome was to have 'preached the kingdom of God', and that is a significant phrase in Acts. It is a phrase which is more normally associated with the gospels; Luke uses it here only occasionally, but positions it at crucial moments in his story. Acts opens with two references to it. Jesus 'appeared to them over a period of forty days and spoke about the kingdom of God' (1:3); in consequence, 'when they met together, they asked him, "Lord, are you at this time going to restore the kingdom to Israel?"' (1:6). It is in that context that Jesus explains the mission to Jerusalem, Judea and Samaria, and the ends of the earth; as we have seen, these are all terms to do with his new kingdom. Similarly, Luke closes his book with two references to the kingdom: the one we have just seen and, a few verses earlier:

> They arranged to meet Paul on a certain day, and came in even larger
> numbers to the place where he was staying. From morning till evening he
> explained and declared to them the kingdom of God and tried to convince
> them about Jesus from the Law of Moses and from the Prophets.
> (28:23)

When the gospel travelled outside a purely Jewish audience for the first time, the Samaritans 'believed Philip as he preached the good news of the kingdom of God and the name of Jesus Christ' (8:12), and one way of describing Paul's regular evangelistic ministry among the Jews was that in Ephesus he 'entered the synagogue and spoke boldly there for three months, arguing persuasively about the kingdom of God' (19:8). Young churches needed to be strengthened with the news that 'We must go through many hardships to enter the kingdom of God' (14:22). And as a mature church was encouraged to follow Paul's pattern, he summed it up in these words to the tearful

Ephesian elders in his farewell speech: 'I know that none of you among whom I have gone about preaching the kingdom will ever see me again' (20:25).

So the kingdom of God is important in Acts, and we see this not from the number of references (a mere eight) but from their significant placing: two at the beginning, two at the end, two in the context of evangelism and two in the context of church leadership. As we shall see later, each of the last four has an important role in Acts as a typical event.

When we ask what the kingdom of God is in Acts, it can be explained only in terms of all the other things that the early church does. Paul was not doing anything different when he explained the kingdom of God to the synagogue in Ephesus contrasted to when he 'proclaimed the word of God in the Jewish synagogues' in Salamis (13:5). In Thessalonica,

> As his custom was, Paul went into the synagogue, and on three Sabbath days he reasoned with them from the Scriptures, explaining and proving that the Christ had to suffer and rise from the dead. 'This Jesus I am proclaiming to you is the Christ,' he said.
>
> (17:2–3)

That was not new either. The kingdom of God is about believing in, and submitting to, the risen Messiah Jesus, our Saviour and Judge. That will need to be unpacked further, but what we must see at this stage is that the kingdom of God is not something other than the message about Jesus.

Putting those two parts of the ending of the book together means that in one important sense it is incomplete, because the task of reaching the ends of the earth with the message of the kingdom of God is incomplete. We find our place in the book here, after it closes. On the other hand, Luke has told us everything he intended to tell us, so in that sense the book is finished and does end with chapter 28; it is finished too in the sense that we now have every piece we need to know for planting and growing churches that will make disciples for Jesus, and of the inevitable suffering that will go with that. So it would be an overstatement to say that we live in 'Acts 29', as if God were concerned with different things today, or had new tasks to give us and new truths to reveal. No: we live, still, in Acts 1–28, because Luke's stated purpose has been to give us *a worldwide, evangelistic message of the kingdom of God for today.*

2. Look for the author's repeated themes

Luke's purposes have already given us one way of breaking the book into logical sections, but in fact there are several, and one of the most useful comes from seeing how a particular repeated theme or phrase occurs. The most obvious in Acts is the pattern of variations on the theme of growth:

> Those who accepted his message were baptised, and about three thousand were added to their number that day. They devoted themselves to the apostles' teaching and to the fellowship, to the breaking of bread and to prayer. Everyone was filled with awe, and many wonders and miraculous signs were done by the apostles. All the believers were together and had everything in common. Selling their possessions and goods, they gave to anyone as he had need. Every day they continued to meet together in the temple courts. They broke bread in their homes and ate together with glad and sincere hearts, praising God and enjoying the favour of all the people. And the Lord added to their number daily those who were being saved. (2:41–47)

> So the word of God spread. The number of disciples in Jerusalem increased rapidly, and a large number of priests became obedient to the faith. (6:7)

> Then the church throughout Judea, Galilee and Samaria enjoyed a time of peace. It was strengthened; and encouraged by the Holy Spirit, it grew in numbers, living in the fear of the Lord. (9:31)

> But the word of God continued to increase and spread. (12:24)

> So the churches were strengthened in the faith and grew daily in numbers. (16:5)

> In this way the word of the Lord spread widely and grew in power. (19:20)

This is not a complete list, because Luke tells us that after the arrest of Peter and John 'many who heard the message believed, and the number of men grew to about five thousand' (4:4). But that is noticed in the middle of a story. What is important about all the examples in the list is that they seem to serve as summary sentences, wrapping up a phase in the narrative and bringing a particular theme to an end:

- 1:1 – 2:47. The first Christians
- 3:1 – 6:7. The first Christians in Jerusalem
- 6:8 – 9:31. The first *partly* Jewish Christians (the Samaritans and a eunuch)
- 9:32 – 12:24. The first *non*-Jewish Christians
- 12:25 – 16:5. The encounter with the wider non-Christian world
- 16:6 – 19:20. More acceptance, more resistance

Since the final part of the story is to do with the gospel reaching Rome, perhaps the last two verses of the book function in the same way:

> For two whole years Paul stayed there in his own rented house and welcomed all who came to see him. Boldly and without hindrance he preached the kingdom of God and taught about the Lord Jesus Christ. (28:30–31)

In that growth the church is not held up as the hero, as if it were solely responsible for its own success. Rather, three of those summary verses say that it was God's word which grew, and that locates the growth in God's plans and effectiveness (6:7; 12:24; 19:20). For those many Christians who live in places of persecution, that is good news, because it is a guarantee that God will honour and prosper his message, irrespective of human or demonic attempts to squash it. To those Christians in an increasingly secular and hostile West, it is a reassurance that God is responsible for his message, and we do not need to dilute it as we try to reach an increasingly distant culture. To those Christians in apparently successful churches, it is a much-needed reminder that true growth comes not from pro-grammes or staffing decisions but from people believing the word of

God. Luke's *repeated theme* is that it is inevitable that true Christianity will grow, even though the price of that may well be the suffering of the Christians.

The architecture *of Acts*

What should be becoming clear is that Luke's narrative is very far from being a casually put together set of memoirs combined with a travel journal. He has written in such a way to make his points clear: writing at a time without variation in font sizes, underlining, paragraphs or chapters, he makes his plan apparent by other methods. Repetition is the most obvious, and it was extremely useful when most Christians would only have heard his book read to them at church, rather than owning it for private study at home. He worked hard to make his message stick. But repetition of phrases was only one of Luke's methods.

It might be helpful to think in terms of the design for the façade of a grand building. Perhaps there are two grand entrances, each with a pair of staircases leading up to them. On another storey the architect has designed a regular series of arches, alternate ones containing a window. A balustrade marks the transition to a third storey, where the surface changes from elegant stone to smooth plasterwork. The more we look at the façade, the more patterns and interrelationships we see, but the building as a whole still has a coherence and makes sense.

So it is with Acts. We have discovered two ways into the architecture of the book, by looking at its opening and closing concerns, and by discovering a phrase which, like the repeated columns of a series of arches, breaks up the whole into a series of smaller, related units. Discovering two, however, does not mean we have done our work. It should prepare us to discover yet more patterns that Luke has prepared in order to teach us.

3. Look for the unique events

Some of the events in Acts have a particular significance because they happen in a very particular place, with a highlight on them. This is a variation of degree, of course – every event is unique – but some seem to have a special role. The election of Matthias as replacement apostle falls into this category (1:12–26), because when James is killed later there is no similar move made to replace him (12:2), nor is Paul elected into his role as apostle. Similarly, the giving of the Holy Spirit at Pentecost is unique. Although it has echoes later on, and the clear assumption is that every Christian has received the Spirit, Luke does not report and does not expect that wind and fire accompanied every conversion.

One of the classic problems in handling Acts is how we discern what is descriptive and what is normative; what is once for all and what is always for everyone. Very often the answer lies within the book, because Luke has not intended to leave his readers helpless. For instance, we have already noted the way the first section of Acts is flooded with Old Testament references and with the motif of fulfil-ment. This can help us handle a story like that of Ananias and Sapphira (5:1–11), because their tale fits into that framework perfectly. There are echoes of the sin of Achan from Joshua 7, in that they 'kept back' money for themselves (5:2), and of Israel's repeated disobedi-ence in the wilderness when they 'test the Spirit of the Lord' (5:9). It is the story in which the word 'church' appears for the first time in Acts (5:11); that word ought to recall the great assembly at Mount Sinai, where God spoke his words to his saved people and expected them to obey him because he would live among them. So Luke is setting Ananias' and Sapphira's rebellion in a framework of the church being the fulfilment of all God's promises to be present among his people. God is real. The early church's generosity, which is the counterpart to the lying couple's meanness, is possibly presented as fulfilment as well, with an echo of Deuteronomy 15:4: 'However, there should be no poor among you, for in the land the LORD your God is giving you to possess as your inheritance, he will richly bless you.' But generosity towards the poor is repeated often enough in Acts (11:28–30; 20:35) to make it clear that it is to be the norm for all Christians. Luke's careful isolation of the *unique events* of the Ananias and Sapphira story within its fulfilment frame, with his careful repetition of the early church's generosity outside it, together show us here what is descriptive and what is normative, provided we pay careful attention.

4. Look for the principal characters
The first human character who claims attention is Peter, who is the dominating figure during chapters 1 – 15. These chapters are

particularly concerned with how the gospel spread from Jew to Gentile, and in various ways Peter's rôle answers the question 'Who may become a Christian?' He was the preacher when the first Jews were converted (2:14–41); he was sent with John to Samaria to authorize the first semi-Jewish conversions (8:14–17); and he was the preacher at the first Gentile conversions following his vision of the end of racial uncleanness (10:1 – 11:18). His preaching ministry in Acts is summarized in his speech to the Jerusalem council: 'Brothers, you know that some time ago God made a choice among you that the Gentiles might hear from my lips the message of the gospel and believe' (15:7). Paying attention to this *principal character* means that we learn that anyone may become a Christian, and that being a Christian means being freed from the demands of the law.

The second principal human character is Paul, and he is continuously present during chapters 9 – 28. There is then some significant overlap between Peter and Paul, but Luke disguises that for a while, until 13:9, because until then he has been called *Saul*. This, presumably, is to introduce him while still allowing Peter to be the main focus for the conversion of Cornelius (10:1 – 11:18) and during his imprisonment and release (12:1–23).

Chapters 9 – 28 are particularly concerned with how the gospel spread from Jerusalem to Rome, and in various ways Paul's role answers the question 'How may we reach the world for Christ?' We learn that it spreads by word of mouth; we see that happening in various places, but with an increasingly familiar method. Paul's strategy in Corinth is typical.

> When Silas and Timothy came from Macedonia, Paul devoted himself exclusively to preaching, testifying to the Jews that Jesus was the Christ. But when the Jews opposed Paul and became abusive, he shook out his clothes in protest and said to them, 'Your blood be on your own heads! I am clear of my responsibility. From now on I will go to the Gentiles.'
>
> Then Paul left the synagogue and went next door to the house of Titius Justus, a worshipper of God. Crispus, the synagogue ruler, and his entire household believed in the Lord; and many of the Corinthians who heard him believed and were baptised.

> One night the Lord spoke to Paul in a vision: 'Do not be afraid; keep on speaking, do not be silent. For I am with you, and no-one is going to attack and harm you, because I have many people in this city.' So Paul stayed for a year and a half, teaching them the word of God.
>
> (18:5–11)

That pattern is typical, because, as Paul argued in Romans 9 – 11, the gospel goes by right to the Jews first, and only on the basis of its rejection by them does it go to the Gentiles. It is also typical because it shows that, although the gospel is fixed and the way of communicating that gospel is by teaching the word of God, the means of delivering it is flexible. Paying attention to *this principal character* shows that Christians think through their evangelism.

Paul's pattern also teaches us that the gospel spreads by the suffering of the Christian, and again Corinth is typical. To continue with the story:

> While Gallio was proconsul of Achaia, the Jews made a united attack on Paul and brought him into court. 'This man,' they charged, 'is persuading the people to worship God in ways contrary to the law.'
>
> Just as Paul was about to speak, Gallio said to the Jews, 'If you Jews were making a complaint about some misdemeanour or serious crime, it would be reasonable for me to listen to you. But since it involves questions about words and names and your own law – settle the matter yourselves. I will not be a judge of such things.' So he had them ejected from the court.
>
> (18:12–16)

What emerges in this section of Acts is that there was increasing Jewish opposition to Paul, increasing Gentile indifference to his fate, and an underscoring of his innocence. This *principal character* teaches us that being a Christian evangelist involves hardship.

These two men are the principals in Acts, and the other apostles are hardly mentioned at all. But the way Luke tells their very different stories is designed to show another factor: their common style of ministry. The similarity in the way Luke finishes their stories has already been noted, but other similarities, listed in Table 2.1, are apparent.

	Peter	Paul
Both heal a lame man	3:2–8	14:8–10
Both do miracles at a distance	5:15	19:12
Both exorcize demonic spirits	5:16	16:16–18
Both confront sorcerers	8:18–24	13:6–11
Both raise the dead	9:36–41	20:9–12
Both have heavenly visions	10:9–16	16:9; 18:9–10; 23:11
Both are miraculously released from prison	5:19; 12:7–11	16:25–28
Both preach to Jews using Psalm 16:10	2:27	13:35

Table 2.1

These similarities, particularly the last one, cannot all be coincidences. Luke is at pains to put these two men on a level: to identify their gospels, their ministries and their common concern for evangelism. These repetitions, to return to the architectural idea, are like a subtle motif that joins two otherwise separate wings of the building. Do not let the differences between the two blind you to their joint apostolic authority and their overlapping concern to make disciples of all nations.

5. Look for God's activities

First of all, the Bible is a book about God. That is obvious but needs stating, because we naturally tend to think that everything revolves around us. So when we read any Bible passage we should ask what it says about God and his character, activity, promises and warnings. It can be a shock to read from that perspective, especially when we discover that one Bible book does not mention God at all.[2]

That is not the issue with Acts, of course. It is the reverse. God is everywhere, and the Holy Spirit alone is mentioned fifty-two times. There have been numerous suggestions that the book be re-titled 'The Acts of the Holy Spirit'.

---

2. It is of course the book of Esther. See Barry G. Webb, *Five Festal Garments* (Leicester: Apollos, 2000), chapter 5, for a helpful reading of it.

When those references are tracked down, though, it becomes apparent they are not spread evenly throughout Acts. The work of the Holy Spirit which Luke comments on seems to occur in clusters:

- The section beginning 1:5 – The commissioning of the twelve apostles, including the replacement for Judas, as they wait for the Spirit.
- The section beginning 2:4 – Pentecost and the first Jewish converts.
- The section beginning 6:3 – The choosing of the seven assistants to free the apostles for their teaching and praying.
- The section beginning 8:17 – The first Samaritan converts.
- The section beginning 10:19 – The first Gentile converts.
- The section beginning 16:6 – The gospel goes to Europe.
- The section beginning 20:23 – Paul's trials and hardships foretold as he travels to evangelize in Jerusalem and Rome.

The fact that the Holy Spirit's work occurs in clusters in Acts should emphasize for us that those events are particularly important. Apart from the first, which is a promise of and preparation for the second, – Pentecost – each cluster can be seen to be about evangelism in some shape or other. So activating this principle highlights for us that the work of the Holy Spirit in Acts is *to push the churches outwards into new missionary activity*, and that this activity is focused on *telling people about Jesus*. Even Peter's sermon at Pentecost is a sermon about Jesus, not about the Holy Spirit.

6. *Look for the stressed teaching*
For a book that is simply called 'Acts', it is surprising to discover how much of it is about words rather than actions. Something like twenty per cent of the book's total length is given over to reporting nineteen speeches, sermons and defences. When those nineteen are analysed, though, a pattern begins to emerge which should not now come as a complete shock: Peter delivers eight, James one, Stephen one, and Paul, again, eight. Once again, Luke has been putting Peter and Paul on an equal footing.

That becomes clearer when two other patterns are observed. The first is that Luke rarely repeats himself. So, although we are told repeatedly that Paul evangelized Jews and Gentiles and that he strengthened the churches, Luke gives us only one of each kind of speech.[3] Going along with those extended speeches are many other one- or two-sentence summaries of the message, which show that it remained the same even though the venue had changed. It would be safe to assume, then, that Luke is telling us that these few full speeches were in many ways typical of the kinds of things that were said to a wide range of people, and that they were said on many occasions. It is not a problem to discover whether Luke took down a particular speech word for word, because in all probability it was one he had heard on many occasions and possibly knew by heart, or could reconstruct from notes.

That can be seen happening in Acts as the second pattern emerges, which is that Luke abbreviates these speeches. Peter's preaching is instructive here. His first full-blown evangelistic sermon is Acts 2:14–36 (twenty-two verses); his second is in 3:12–26 (fourteen verses); his third is 4:8–11; 19–20 (five verses); then 5:29–32 (three verses), and so on. The verse numberings are new, but the decreasing length is clear. As Luke increasingly abbreviates Peter's sermons, it becomes apparent that he is stripping Peter's message down to its barest essentials; 5:29–32 shows this clearly:

We must obey God rather than men! The God of our fathers raised Jesus from the dead – whom you had killed by hanging him on a tree. God exalted him to his own right hand as Prince and Saviour that he might give repentance and forgiveness of sins to Israel. We are witnesses of these things, and so is the Holy Spirit, whom God has given to those who obey him.

That has condensed into a simple three-headed message about Jesus: *You* killed him; *God* raised him; *we* saw him. When the message went to those who were not at the crucifixion, in 10:36–41, Peter adapted it slightly:

You know the message God sent to the people of Israel, telling the good news of peace through Jesus Christ, who is Lord of all. You know what has happened throughout Judea, beginning in Galilee after the baptism that John

---

3. Jews 13:16–41; Gentiles 17:22–31 (although 14:14–17 might count as a speech to a different kind of audience); churches 20:18–35.

preached – how God anointed Jesus of Nazareth with the Holy Spirit and power, and how he went around doing good and healing all who were under the power of the devil, because God was with him.

We are witnesses of everything he did in the country of the Jews and in Jerusalem. They killed him by hanging him on a tree, but God raised him from the dead on the third day and caused him to be seen. He was not seen by all the people, but by witnesses whom God had already chosen – by us who ate and drank with him after he rose from the dead.

The threefold message is now fourfold. There is first some information about Jesus, because Cornelius and his people would have been ignorant about that, and then it becomes *they* (not *you*) killed him, *God* raised him, *we* saw him, followed by the same call to repent and believe and the same offer of forgiveness and the Holy Spirit. The brevity of the last part of the sermon, compared with the extended information about Jesus, when we couple it with Luke's standard abbreviating style, means that what he is giving us here is a brief note that it is the same message which needs to go to Gentiles as well as Jews, but that those who know nothing require a longer introduction into Jesus and his life and teaching.

The same move emerges one stage further when Paul preaches to Jews and Gentiles in a synagogue, in 13:16–42. There is here a longer Old Testament background to the message, to provide the context for Jesus' Messiahship, and the same kind of material about the historical Jesus. But when he arrives at the crucifixion, Paul says (vv. 26–31):

Brothers, children of Abraham, and you God-fearing Gentiles, it is to us that this message of salvation has been sent. The people of Jerusalem and their rulers did not recognise Jesus, yet in condemning him they fulfilled the words of the prophets that are read every Sabbath. Though they found no proper ground for a death sentence, they asked Pilate to have him executed. When they had carried out all that was written about him, they took him down from the tree and laid him in a tomb. But God raised him from the dead, and for many days he was seen by those who had travelled with him from Galilee to Jerusalem. They are now his witnesses to our people.

The pattern has now become *they* (not *you*) killed him; *God* raised him; *they* (not *we*) saw him. Finally, Luke has directed us to the form of the gospel that can be preached to any person at any time in any place, and he has shown us, in stages, that it is the same gospel that Peter preached at Pentecost. Christians, then, believe a fixed and surprisingly simple message that can be adopted and adapted to any culture and any degree of prior knowledge, yet without compromising those core beliefs.[4] Applying this principle of comparing the speeches has given us *the pattern for our own evangelistic message.*

The exception to that pattern seems to be in the speeches Paul makes before his various trials and hearings. There is consistent overlap and repetition here, and perhaps Luke wants to underline Paul's testimony to make a very particular point, over whether Paul was guilty or innocent in law. It would have made a major impact on the reception of the gospel among non-Christians, and even caused committed Christians to distance themselves from him.[5]

Speeches also give a window into the big picture of Acts, because what could be seen as the two most important speeches – Peter's on the Day of Pentecost in chapter 2 and James's at the Council of Jerusalem in chapter 15 – share a common feature in their use of the Old Testament. Peter (2:17–36) expounds Joel 2:28–32, and this becomes the dominating passage not only for his sermon but arguably for the first half of the book, as the motif of the giving of the Spirit to all is explored. That might explain the motif of 'signs' and 'wonders', which, while superficially very common in Acts, is only present in the first half. The words do not appear after the Council of Jerusalem. James (15:13–21) expounds Amos 9:11–12 and the message there about the inclusion of the Gentiles. Although the first Gentile has already been converted, and the Council has heard

---

4. The pattern of condensing what Luke has told us before, and only expanding on what is new, explains the otherwise odd shape of Paul's speech in Athens (17:22–31), which only glances at the resurrection, yet provokes a strong reaction. Presumably we are to understand that what Paul said at that point is what he always said at that point, which Luke has already told us (13:32–41).

5. 2 Tim. 4:16.

evidence from the first Gentile mission, it is the refusal to place
barriers in the way of Gentile converts which lifts the lid on what
follows, with a wholehearted backing of what Paul and his companions are doing. Peter now slips from the scene, as does James,
and Paul's ministry is the central focus for the second half of the
book.

7. Look for the biblical setting

The biblical setting of Acts is so obvious that it is easy to underestimate. But, just as we always read the Old Testament with the
knowledge that our understanding of it is incomplete and dis-
torted unless we place Jesus at its centre,[6] so we must read Acts as
the continuing work of the risen and ascended Jesus who was crucified.

The linking between the two books is obviously vital for examin-
ing themes that bridge the two, like the cross. Luke's theology
reaches its clearest expression in Acts after Pentecost, so much so that
developing the theme from Luke without running it on into Acts
runs the risk of misrepresenting Luke's intention. By the same logic,
a theme like the cross requires the theology of the gospel to flesh it
out, before we allow Acts to give it the distinctive element of how it
is fulfilled in the preaching of the gospel.

The principle of looking at the biblical setting gives a second angle
here, too. Since Luke highlighted 'the things that have been fulfilled
among us' (Luke 1:1) as a major concern, we can trace the fulfilment
of the Old Testament through both books as one long exploration of
the issue. The theme in Luke and Acts could be sketched out like
this:

• Jesus remakes the nation of Israel (Luke 6:12–16)
• Jesus remakes the exodus (Luke 9:31)[7]
• Jesus remakes the Passover (Luke 22:14–23)
• Jesus remakes the kingdom (Acts 1:3, 6, 8)
• Jesus remakes Sinai/Pentecost (Acts 2:1–13)

---

6. Luke 24:13–49 underlines that twice.

7. The Greek for 'departure' is the same as 'exodus'.

followed by three desert experiences:

- Jesus remakes the covenantal blessing (Acts 4:34; cf. Deut. 15:4)
- Jesus remakes the covenantal curse (Acts 5:1–11; cf. Josh. 7)
- Jesus remakes the government of his people (Acts 6:1–7; cf. Exod. 18:17–23)

This principle shows us that *the continuing story of Jesus is one with deep Old Testament roots*, which needs clear knowledge of God's dealings with his people in order to understand it correctly.

An example of that is the idea of 'signs', or 'signs and wonders', that occurs several times in Acts. Peter, in his Pentecost sermon, said that Joel prophesied them (2:19) and Jesus did them (2:22); Luke then reports that the apostles did them too (2:43). The early church prayed for God to perform them through Jesus (4:30), and subsequently the apostles (5:12), senior Christians (6:8; 8:6, 13) and Paul and Barnabas (14:3; 15:12) performed them. What may not be apparent from this is that there is a large Old Testament background to the term, which Peter referred to in Joel, and which Stephen specifically mentions in his speech as well (7:36). Overwhelmingly there is one reference point.

A *sign* in the Old Testament was sometimes a mark of God's covenant promises being kept,[8] or simply a mark of his presence.[9] It might be miraculous,[10] or non-miraculous (like circumcision), although a *wonder* was usually a miracle. The performance of a 'sign' or 'wonder' was no guarantee that God was behind the performer, and the Israelites were warned to watch out for those who perform them and then teach lies about God.[11] Signs accompanied God's people into exile in Babylon[12] and were a longed-for indication of the arrival of God's new kingdom, which is how Peter understood Joel. But all those points are on the edge of, or derive from, the main definition.

---

8. Gen. 9:12.
9. Judg. 6:17.
10. Isa. 7:14.
11. Deut. 13:1–5.
12. Ezekiel has this as a particular note: see Ezek. 24:24.

'Signs and wonders' were the miraculous acts God performed as he delivered his people from bondage in Egypt, and around two-thirds of the references to the concept have the Exodus in view.[13] This means that the concepts are highly charged and, when coupled together, indicate that God is doing something as important in saving history as the Exodus. When Peter said that Jesus was 'a man accredited by God . . . by miracles, wonders and signs' (2:22), he was saying far more than that Jesus performed miracles, which would have been wonderful enough. He was claiming that Jesus' life, death and resurrection were being attested by God as saving events on the eternal time plan. Consequently, when people in Acts are enabled to perform 'wonders and miraculous signs' (2:43), Luke is teaching us that what they were part of was more than a healing ministry. The events in Acts are a continuation of the saving plan, and God attests that by the giving of *signs*.

This may help further in working out what in Acts is descriptive and what is normative, for there are no great saving events occurring today that God needs to attest. Of course people are being saved today, and of course there are miracles today, but neither has the biblically important title of *sign* or *wonder*, because nothing that happens today is breaking new ground in the way that Pentecost did.

8. Look for the positional context
Many of the principles hover around the issue of context. As we understand Luke's story as a whole as it develops, we can see how each story plays its part; and just as we understand God's grand plan through the whole of the Bible, we can see how Acts plays its part.

---

13. Consulting a reliable concordance will show that fourteen of the thirty-six references to *môpēt* (marvel, sign) occur directly in the narratives around the Exodus, and seven more look back to it (Neh. 9:10; Pss. 78:43; 105:27 and therefore v. 5; Ps. 135:9; Jer. 32:20, 21). Thirty-three out of seventy-nine occurrences of its near-synonym *'ôt* (sign, mark) occur in the Exodus context, and five more look back (Josh. 24:17; Neh. 9:10; Pss. 78:43; 105:27; 135:9; Jer. 32:21). Only twice in Exodus God does a 'wonder' (*pl'*) (Exod. 3:20; 34:10, although see 15:11), but overwhelmingly elsewhere the term is used for looking back and remembering God's redeeming acts.

That principle applies on the level of the developing nature of Luke's story as he gradually unfolds and explains his teaching over several successive and carefully positioned stories. Two examples might help.

Ananias and Sapphira (5:1–11)

We have already seen in Principle 3 that the story of Ananias and Sapphira is made much clearer when we see that it happens in the part of the book which is flooded with Old Testament allusions and the motif of fulfilment. We also need, though, to see how Luke leads up to the story. In 4:32–35 he shows the normal pattern of the early church, which was one of generosity. It is clear that no-one was compelled to give up all their possessions, but that in a spirit of love 'from time to time, as anyone had need' people would give out of their capital rather than their income. That alone is a rebuke to the Western churches today.

The next scene (4:36–37) shines the spotlight on one such individual, Barnabas. It does not add anything to the information (apart from introducing Barnabas, who will be important later in the story), but it does give a glimpse of one generous individual to prepare us for the next scene of two falsely generous individuals. What Luke is doing in the first two scenes is painting the background, in general and in detail, to the third. He also prevents us from misreading the third story. Did Ananias and Sapphira have to do this? No. Were they required to sell everything they owned? No. Did they have to do it at that time? No. In other words, their lie was premeditated and unforced. They wanted the same kind of approval that Barnabas had.

Philip and the Ethiopian (8:26–40)

This story is significant for a number of reasons, which become sharper when the story is placed alongside its partner, the ministry of Philip in Samaria (8:4–8) and, in particular, the challenge to his ministry by Simon Magus. Behind all of them lies the persecution of the church in Jerusalem and its spread around Judea and Samaria, which means that the apostles, who remain in Jerusalem (8:1), can no longer be the carriers of the message. This raises the fundamental problem which the stories surrounding Philip solve: how can the gospel spread without the authorizing presence of the apostles?

The stories which follow answer this in two ways. Philip, who is manifestly not an apostle (6:5), takes the same message, with the same signs, and people are genuinely converted and baptized (8:12). But the non-apostolic nature of Philip's ministry creates a tension, because he, and the other Christians, have been preaching in Samaria to those who were not fully, or properly, Jews. This is the second move that Jesus predicted in 1:8: that they should go to Judea and Samaria. Such a major move needs to be authorized by the apostles, which is why there is a close monitoring and visit (8:14–17) and the subsequent gift of the Holy Spirit. The oddity that the converts believe and are baptized but do not receive the Spirit should be understood in this way.

The partner story makes this clear, because the Ethiopian is a eunuch (8:27) and therefore barred from the worship in the temple where he had just visited.[14] What is striking in this story, when compared with that of the Samaritan Christians, is how little contact the man has with Philip. They meet in the middle of the desert and part shortly afterwards, the man having heard the gospel and come to faith. To put it more sharply, he has, like the Samaritans, heard about Jesus Christ from Philip (8:5, 35) and been baptized by him (8:38). But this time there is no apostolic visit or gift of the Spirit. In fact, it looks as if Luke is at pains to show that there could not have been, as the man returns to spiritual isolation in Ethiopia. This pairing has been highlighted for us by Luke to show that there was no need for a second visit by the apostles. Once was enough, and it is now permissible for non-apostles to convert and baptize outside the strict racial boundary of the Jewish people. The non-repetition authorizes us to do the same today.

The second way these stories show how the gospel can spread without the authorizing presence of the apostles lies in the message, and it can be seen in contrasting the ministries of Philip and Simon. Luke has used repetition to show that the content of Philip's gospel was the same as the apostles'. Like them he talks of Jesus Christ and his kingdom (8:5, 12, 35). The contrast with Simon Magus lies in the focus of the message, because Simon 'boasted he was someone great' (8:9) who wanted to be known as the 'Great Power' (8:10), and

---

14. Deut. 23:1.

that was the essence of why he was more fascinated by Philip's and the apostles' miracles rather than their message. By contrast, the passage of Isaiah that Philip expounds to the eunuch is not about greatness at all – or at least, not the kind of greatness that fascinated Simon – but of weakness and 'humiliation' (8:33). In God's providence, that casual conversation serves as a crucial clarifying moment as the church moves out of purely Jewish membership and asks itself what kind of Messiah it will present to a lost Gentile world. Philip would tell us that it is the same Messiah that the apostles presented: the one who was crucified in weakness for our sins (see below, pp. 68–72).

So Luke's careful arrangement has again shown how he teaches his readers vital truths. He has shown us the reality of the nature of the church and the reality of the imperative of evangelism. He has also begun to show by this careful pairing which elements of his story are to be understood as for all Christians everywhere, and which are unique to his day. Clearly, he would not be happy either with bringing everything across to today, or with locking the book into a long-lost historical moment. The principle of looking to the *positional context* means that he has not left us to flounder on the question, but has shown us himself how to take the move to our day.

What kind of book is Acts?

Historical

This is the most obvious level on which Acts operates, and there are events here which we simply would not know about if this book did not exist. It would be impossible to construct Paul's travels and trials, or even the spread of the gospel, without the information here. But this obvious level is also the least interesting, at least to Luke. Of course, the events are historical, but Luke is not attempting to write a complete history of the early church. There are too many gaps and odd emphases. So, while the historical side is useful – for instance, in terms of providing a grid against which the New Testament letters can often be placed, or giving historical notes which can be checked against what historians know from elsewhere and so contribute to a wider field of knowledge – we should not make this the sole point of interest in the book.

Theological

Combining the substantial material from the speeches, and then noting the careful way Luke structures the narrative, shows that this is a theological book. Acts will teach us, over and again, the heart of the gospel: the death and resurrection of Jesus. It will teach us what may need to be changed, and what is transferable from culture to culture: repentance and faith. It will teach us the results of the gospel: forgiveness and the gift of the Holy Spirit.

Because of its intimate connection with Luke's Gospel, we should also allow the two to work together. So from the Gospel we can draw much more detail about Jesus' life and teaching. From Acts we can draw more detail about the meaning of Jesus' death and resurrection, as their implications are spelled out and thought through. Allowing the two books to teach us together will give their message even greater clarity.

Missionary

Thirdly, we should see how Luke teaches us the methods of being an obedient missionary, learning lessons from the apostles while not confusing ourselves with them. So we can begin to discern a strategy in Paul's focus on cities and towns – the differing kinds of presentation to differing audiences – while still seeing the core message faithfully maintained. We learn from expert missionaries.

We also learn from them that this is no mere textbook exercise or slick manual for church growth that guarantees results. There is opposition: both human and supernatural, both within and beyond the church. There is the need to pray and for dependence on God's Spirit, who may not lead us to the most common-sense plan of action (16:7), but for the sake of his glory may take us by another route to greater fruitfulness (16:9) or greater suffering (20:23). There is also the deep reality that, however much faithful people work, only God can convert people (16:13–14).

Training

As we learn, by studying the missionary strategy, we are being taught how to be trained to plant and lead churches in a way that honours God. Starting the work in Lystra, Derbe, Antioch and Iconium required missionaries to 'preach the good news' (14:7).

Establishing those churches required further work, as Paul and Barnabas

> returned to Lystra, Iconium and Antioch, strengthening the disciples and
> encouraging them to remain true to the faith. 'We must go through many
> hardships to enter the kingdom of God,' they said. Paul and Barnabas
> appointed elders for them in each church and, with prayer and fasting, com-
> mitted them to the Lord, in whom they had put their trust.
> (14:21–23)

In the same way, we are allowed to watch in detail as Paul trains and uses Timothy, and then Luke uses his familiar pattern of abbreviated repetition to indicate that the same method was used with many other future leaders.

One element of Acts, then, is that it is a training manual, but only when we have understood the theological heart of it. It would play down the issue too much to say that the training of future leaders is a side issue within Acts – Luke puts too much emphasis on it for that – but it is not prominent enough to make it central. What is central is the gospel; training future leaders who can teach it faithfully to people who are not yet believers is a necessary implication of that message.[15]

Where now?

The next stage in understanding Acts is to divide it up into more manageable sections, and the best way of doing that is probably to follow Luke's division markers on the theme of growth (2:46–47; 6:7; 9:31; 12:24; 16:5; 19:20; 28:30–31). Each of those sections is too long for a sermon, of course, but it will allow us to see whether there are common concerns in each section that help the stories to fit together, and also to get a sense of the series of movements within the book. It

---

15. The classic texts on this area remain Roland Allen's two books *Missionary Methods: St. Paul's and Ours* (first published in 1912) and *The Spontaneous Expansion of the Church and the Causes which Hinder it* (first published in 1927).

is dangerously easy with Acts to have the impression that there is a large number of exciting stories which happened in a particular order, but if they had happened in any other order it would not have mattered, and once we get to the exciting spread of the gospel after chapter 10, then it does not matter how we shuffle the pack and deal them. That is not safe and it is not wise. Luke has told us that he has written an 'orderly account' (Luke 1:3), and we should pay close attention to that.

Part II: Studying Acts

3 | The first believers: 1:1 – 2:47

Luke and Acts are a historical and theological unity with issues flowing from one to the other. But they are also two separate books, roughly the same length and covering the same time span: just over thirty years. Both begin in very similar ways, with people waiting for something to happen, and raising issues that the book as a whole will answer. Without wishing to force this too far, there does seem to be a deliberate pattern in the first few pages, as can be seen from Table 3.1.

Luke	Acts	
1:1–4	1:1–5	Why is Luke writing this book?
1:5 – 2:52	1:6–26	Preparations
3:1 – 4:13	2:1–41	Equipping for ministry by the Holy Spirit
4:14–15	2:42–47	Summary of ministry
4:16–end	3:1–end	Ministry

Table 3.1

It is an intriguing parallel and certainly emphasizes that this section has a central theme: the waiting for and arrival of the Holy Spirit, and the result of his coming, which is the witness to Jesus.

Why is Luke writing? 1:1–5

There are four main elements to these verses, which taken together show how Luke thought Christianity should function; it is how he carefully describes the church in the first, Jerusalem-based section which follows (1:6 – 2:47).

The command to witness to the King

The risen Jesus gave both 'instructions' and 'many convincing proofs' to the apostles as he 'spoke about the kingdom of God' (1:2–3). Throughout Luke's Gospel, Jesus had talked of God's kingdom as an ever-growing, unconquerable source of blessing for all nations. At one point he had asked:

> 'What is the kingdom of God like? What shall I compare it to? It is like a mustard seed, which a man took and planted in his garden. It grew and became a tree, and the birds of the air perched in its branches.'
>
> Again he asked, 'What shall I compare the kingdom of God to? It is like yeast that a woman took and mixed into a large amount of flour until it worked all through the dough.'
> (Luke 13:18–21)

Just as here, throughout the Gospel there is a sense of delayed excitement, because certain things must be in place before the kingdom can be fully announced. Once those things have happened, though, and the King has been enthroned, the message of the kingdom will circle the world. Here in Acts there is a feeling that, finally, all the elements are in place.

The power of the Holy Spirit

Surely, the disciples must have thought, we are now fully persuaded that Jesus has risen from the dead and fully committed to telling everyone about him. What is to hold us back? Jesus insists, however, that they should 'wait for the gift' of the Holy Spirit (1:4), and this looks back to two key moments in Luke's Gospel.

At the beginning of Jesus' ministry, John the Baptist had said, 'I baptise you with water. But one more powerful than I will come, the thongs of whose sandals I am not worthy to untie. He will baptise you with the Holy Spirit and with fire' (Luke 3:16). Jesus' reference to that prophecy here is underlined by his almost-fulfilled promise that 'in a few days you will be baptised with the Holy Spirit' (1:5). Similarly, at the end of Jesus' earthly ministry he had made the promise which either he remade here, or Luke records for us a second time. He told his disciples:

> This is what is written: The Christ will suffer and rise from the dead on the
> third day, and repentance and forgiveness of sins will be preached in his name
> to all nations, beginning at Jerusalem. You are witnesses of these things. I am
> going to send you what my Father has promised; but stay in the city until
> you have been clothed with power from on high.
>
> (Luke 24:46–49)

Both in Luke and here in Acts, Jesus underlines his and the Father's joint work in sending the Holy Spirit. The preaching of the kingdom of God, then, cannot be achieved by mere human effort, but requires the work of the Father, Son and Holy Spirit to accomplish it.

The rôle of the apostles

The command to *witness* has often been taken as if it meant to tell people about the Christian message, or even to share one's own testimony. But it is clear that Jesus meant something very particular, for these eleven men were to be, as he puts it, 'my witnesses'. They were to give testimony to Jesus' story, rather than their own story, and, as becomes clear when they need to replace Judas, they were to have been people who were witnesses to Jesus' life, death and resurrection.

That has an immediate implication for thinking clearly about our own evangelism, for none of us can give the same first-hand testimony as these men, for the simple reason that none of us saw, heard and understood what they did. However precious our own experiences of God, they are not simply on a different scale to those of the apostles, but of a different kind. When we talk about the empty tomb, or the raising of Lazarus, we are at best only second-hand witnesses. These were the men who knew Jesus before his death, and so could justifiably claim to recognize him after his resurrection.

The continuing work of Jesus

Luke has already told his readers that volume 1 of his work dealt with what Jesus 'began to do and to teach', and so we would be justified in expecting that volume 2 will explore what Jesus continued to do and to teach. The focus, then, will lie not on the church's growing understanding of the implications of what Jesus had achieved, so much as on his gradual unfolding of the implications of it. Once he had ascended to heaven, Jesus did not end his work and leave the church to its own devices; he continued to guide its developing faith.

Four preparatory elements: 1:6 – 2:13

These four elements circle around, in this opening section of Acts, as Luke's main concerns. At times they change their order and overlap, but they provide a reasonably reliable framework to follow until we reach 2:13.

The command to witness to the King: 1:6–8

Since Jesus has been talking to them about the 'kingdom of God' (v. 3), the disciples' question in verse 6 is quite natural, and possibly understandably impatient. 'Lord, are you at this time going to restore the kingdom to Israel?' That has been an obvious issue since Jesus had taken Isaiah's promises about the future blessings of God's reign and applied them directly to his own ministry. 'Today', he had said, 'this scripture is fulfilled in your hearing' (Luke 4:21).

That day of blessing had continued for three years, but everyone knew that one day God's patience with those who refuse to submit to his kingly rule would run out, and that he would finally enforce his justice. That Jesus had claimed to be agent of both the blessing and the judgment only made the period of waiting more intense. The disciples were effectively asking whether it was time for the end of the world, the day of judgment, the vindication of God and his righteous people.

To this Jesus' answer is that they have not really understood the nature of the kingdom, and that much of what God had intended to achieve on the last day he has already achieved in the death, resurrection and (shortly) ascension to glory of King Jesus.

How much has been achieved can be seen in the new work that lies ahead of them: to go to the nations and witness to his kingly rule. These geographical notes are often taken as giving us a useful way into the structure of Acts: the gospel goes first to Jerusalem (chapters 1 – 7); then to Judea and Samaria (chapters 8 – 15); and then to the ends of the earth (which might mean Rome; or Spain; or all the points of the compass). That is all true; but we need to see first that they are theological markers before they are geographical or stylistic ones, and that the common theological element is the kingdom.

Jerusalem was, first and foremost, the City of David (2 Sam. 5:9), the King, who reigned and was buried there (1 Kgs 2:10). As Peter was soon to say in the heart of Jerusalem, 'David died and was buried, and his tomb is here to this day' (Acts 2:29). All the subsequent kings of Judah reigned from Jerusalem, and it was there that King Zedekiah mounted the final attempt to resist the armies of Babylon (2 Kgs 24:20 – 25:7). The longings of God's people for God to keep his covenant promise and restore the line of Davidic kings is a frequent element in the Old Testament at this stage, as is God's reassurance that he will keep his word.

> For this is what the LORD says: 'David will never fail to have a man to sit on the throne of the house of Israel, nor will the priests, who are Levites, ever fail to have a man to stand before me continually to offer burnt offerings, to burn grain offerings and to present sacrifices.'
>
> (Jer. 33:17–18)

So, when Jesus says that his kingdom will be announced first of all in Jerusalem, we should remember that this was the most natural place for such an event to occur, if he was who he claimed. Where else should the Davidic King announce his kingdom?

But that inheritance was a troubled and divided one. The last king to reign over an undivided kingdom was David's son Solomon; long before King Zedekiah the nation had split into two independent but fiercely competitive nations, with rival temple cults and claimants for the throne. Where the line of descent of the kings of Judah in Jerusalem passed from generation to generation, the crown of the northern kingdom, Israel (or Samaria), was passed on through betrayal, murder and ambition. Comparing the two kingdoms in 1 and 2 Kings and 1 and 2 Chronicles, it becomes clear that however rebellious David's descendants were, God never forgot his covenantal and dynastic promise to them. But those who had rebelled against them were rebelling against God. Their departure into exile was earlier and far more complete.

How wonderful, then, that the next area where Jesus' kingdom is to be announced is in Judea and Samaria, the two halves of that divided kingdom. Jesus, then, was to have a kingdom that would restore these warring factions, and fulfil the promises of restoration. As Ezekiel had foretold:

The word of the LORD came to me: 'Son of man, take a stick of wood and write on it, "Belonging to Judah and the Israelites associated with him." Then take another stick of wood, and write on it, "Ephraim's stick, belonging to Joseph and all the house of Israel associated with him." Join them together into one stick so that they will become one in your hand.

When your countrymen ask you, "Won't you tell us what you mean by this?" say to them, "This is what the Sovereign LORD says: I am going to take the stick of Joseph – which is in Ephraim's hand – and of the Israelite tribes associated with him, and join it to Judah's stick, making them a single stick of wood, and they will become one in my hand." Hold before their eyes the sticks you have written on and say to them, "This is what the Sovereign LORD says: I will take the Israelites out of the nations where they have gone. I will gather them from all around and bring them back into their own land. I will make them one nation in the land, on the mountains of Israel. There will be one king over all of them and they will never again be two nations or be divided into two kingdoms. They will no longer defile themselves with their idols and vile images or with any of their offences, for I will save them from all their sinful backsliding, and I will cleanse them. They will be my people, and I will be their God.

'"My servant David will be king over them, and they will all have one shepherd. They will follow my laws and be careful to keep my decrees. They will live in the land I gave to my servant Jacob, the land where your fathers lived. They and their children and their children's children will live there for

ever, and David my servant will be their prince for ever. I will make a
covenant of peace with them; it will be an everlasting covenant. I will
establish them and increase their numbers, and I will put my sanctuary
among them for ever. My dwelling-place will be with them; I will be their
God, and they will be my people. Then the nations will know that I the LORD
make Israel holy, when my sanctuary is among them for ever."'
(Ezek. 37:15–28)

The mention of the nations in that final verse gives us the third
theological and geographical marker, because God's claim in the Old
Testament was never limited merely to Israel or Judah. As Isaiah
recorded of God's commissioning of his servant,

> It is too small a thing for you to be my servant
> to restore the tribes of Jacob
> and bring back those of Israel I have kept.
> I will also make you a light for the Gentiles,
> that you may bring my salvation to the ends of the earth.
> (Isa. 49:6; cf. Acts 13:47)

So the disciples know that God's kingdom still has work for them
to do, and that until the times and dates the Father has set by his own
authority (which still lie in the future), they are to wait until the Spirit
comes on them with power and then to leave Jerusalem to witness to
the world of its King.

The continuing work of Jesus Christ: 1:9–11
God's glory was frequently masked by cloud, as at Mount Sinai
(Exod. 19:9 etc.); in the tabernacle (Lev. 16:2); and in the temple (1 Kgs
8:10). So Jesus' ascent into the cloud here must be taken as meaning
that he moved to the centre of God's glory, unafraid and uncon-
sumed. Four times the disciples are told where he is; both 'sky' (vv.
10–11) and 'heaven' (v. 11) translate the same Greek word. He is in the
place of supreme authority. Will he always remain there? No, for he
will return in the same way he has departed; presumably his concern
then will be to see how his command to witness to the world has
been completed.
In other words, the task of evangelism is what will uniquely define

and characterize the gospel age, the church age, the time of the heavenly reign of Jesus and the earthly task of his people. The present place, rôle and work of Jesus are a second continuing motif in Acts; both Stephen before his death (7:56) and Paul at his conversion encounter Jesus enthroned in glory.

So, if the geographical marker of 1:8 is also a theological marker, the theological marker here is also a geographical one, because it places Jesus as supreme King over every continent, class and culture.

The rôle of the apostles: 1:12–26

In obedience to Jesus' command to wait, the eleven apostles return to their lodging in Jerusalem. The Holy Spirit's coming will enable them to obey Jesus' command to leave it. When they arrive they come together; so that we do not miss the point of what is about to occur, Luke carefully lists those present. The group is wider than the apostles (1:14), but comparing the names with Luke's previous list (Luke 6:14–16) shows the glaring omission of Judas. They had been twelve, symbolically the new Israel, but now that hope appears to be shattered. How can the witness to the old Israel work if it is so obviously incomplete? So they seek to replace Judas.

Peter bases this on two Psalms that are to do with betrayal. Both are taken elsewhere in the New Testament as Messianic, fitting the pattern of the suffering but subsequently victorious king, and it was obviously a natural development to see the king's betrayer in the Psalms as Judas. It was within God's plan for Judas to lose his place (Ps. 69:25) and within God's plan for another to take it (Ps. 109:8). Judas' betrayal has not wrecked God's plan, and the logic of that will be applied with even greater force to Jesus' death in chapter 2.

There are three elements to being the needed replacement apostle. The first two are easily met, because he must 'have been with us the whole time the Lord Jesus went in and out among us', and be 'a witness with us of his resurrection' (vv. 21–22). Notice the meaning of 'witness' again, because this person will be required to give public testimony of the reality of Jesus' physical resurrection. There would have been quite a sizeable number of people in that category, even if Peter does intend to narrow the field down to men (1:21). Paul mentions that more than five hundred people had seen the risen Jesus and (by implication) were willing to state that publicly (1 Cor. 15:6), and a good number of them would have been among the crowds that accompanied Jesus.

That is not enough to be the replacement for Judas, of course, and here the third element comes into play, because the person must be personally commissioned by Jesus. They choose two men who are likely candidates and ask Jesus to 'show us which of these two you have chosen' (v. 24). It is, then, Jesus' choice, not that of the church.

The action of casting lots has caused many readers unease. Should the eleven not have waited for Pentecost, when, with the Holy Spirit's help, they would have known by a word of prophecy? Should they not have waited for the conversion of Paul, who was clearly in Jesus' mind all along, rather than the quickly forgotten Matthias? Should they not have done something more 'spiritual' than casting lots?

But those qualms show that we have not really grasped the unique moment in the church's history that this scene represents. The New Israel needed twelve members on whom the Spirit would fall, and they needed to be twelve in order to witness to the old Israel immediately. The casting of lots, far from being pagan, was a deeply biblical way of behaving as the trusting people of God; it was how Joshua had arranged for the land to be divided between the twelve tribes (Josh. 18:10). What is remarkable is that the church sees Jesus to be in such a position of almighty power that he can control this seemingly random event. As Proverbs says (16:33):

> The lot is cast into the lap,
>   but its every decision is from the LORD.

The early church was evidently identifying Jesus in that Lordly role. The apostles, then, cannot appoint apostles, because that is Jesus' prerogative. They make the number up to thirteen, and Jesus narrows it down to twelve.

This unprecedented and unrepeated episode underscores the nature of the apostles' authority: they are Jesus' personally commissioned eyewitnesses of his life and resurrection. There must be, and can only be, twelve of them; which is, presumably, why James is not replaced after his execution (12:2).

The power of the Holy Spirit: 2:13

Pentecost was the harvest festival for Israel (Num. 28:26): a solemn assembly of the whole people to be celebrated fifty days after Passover (Lev. 23:15–16). Hence the name, from the Greek word for fifty, *pentē*; possibly we are supposed to see the first converts in 2:41 as a kind of first-fruits celebration, anticipating the full harvest that is to come throughout the rest of the church's history. But it was also the day on which the great assembly of Sinai was thought to have taken place (Exod. 19:1), and it is intriguing to notice the parallels of wind / Spirit, fire and the message, which at Sinai made people beg for it to cease (Exod. 20:19; Heb. 12:19) and which in Acts has people begging for more (Acts 2:37). It is tempting to parallel the giving of the Law with the giving of the Spirit, and to note with Jeremiah that the new Covenant, in contrast to Sinai, is internal not external and based on Spirit not Law (Jer. 31:31–34).

Those echoes, if they are there, are all underneath. What lies on the surface is that the Holy Spirit equips the twelve for world evangelization. The speaking in other tongues (2:4) is a Spirit-given ability to communicate with perfect clarity in a previously unknown language, the languages of every nation (2:5). That breathtaking phrase is, of course, made from a Jewish and Old Testament perspective, where it is, once more, a theological rather than merely an ethnographical note (Isa. 49:6). What looked on the surface like a gathering of mutually incomprehensible strangers from around the Mediterranean and beyond turns out to be a foretaste of the great assembly in heaven – the 'great multitude that no-one could count, from every nation, tribe, people and language' (Rev. 7:9) – all there because there is the eternal gospel to proclaim to those who live on the earth: to 'every nation, tribe, language and people' (Rev. 14:6).

Putting it together

The four key elements that were outlined in 1:1–5 have now been put in place. Luke has shown the complete number of apostles, equipped by the Holy Spirit to witness to the world concerning the crucified, risen, reigning and returning King Jesus. The next event is dazzlingly inevitable: Peter, as the leading apostle, preaches the first evangelistic sermon, and he does it representatively to the whole world, starting in Jerusalem.

Peter's Pentecost sermon: 2:14–41

As is often the case with speeches and letters in the New Testament, Peter's sermon is very carefully constructed to lead towards a particular conclusion, which is the statement in 2:36: 'God has made this Jesus, whom you crucified, both Lord and Christ.' Both titles, Lord and Christ, will be argued for biblically, and the resurrection will be explained in relation to them.

Those days and these days
Peter begins by explaining the speaking in tongues (which, remember, each person heard not as a confusing sound of other languages but – remarkably – as comprehensible speech in his or her own language (2:6)) as God's promise-keeping act. He opens with a quotation from Joel 2:28–32: a prophecy of those days which Peter, rightly, calls the Last Days. It was a time which Joel saw in the dim future; there were various events that he prophesied would happen first, and only afterwards would these things occur. But what Joel saw as distant future, Peter sees as happening before their eyes, because this is what was spoken by Joel (v. 16). These are the Last Days, and they are marked by men and women, young and old, bearing witness to the fact that God's clock has moved on; Jesus' resurrection, ascension and giving of the Spirit mean that a new era has begun. That is the nature and content of their prophecy. Just like Joel, they foresee that God will act in the Last Days, but what Joel saw happening in those days they now identify as what Peter will later call 'these days' (3:24). The prophecy and dreams and visions, together with the blood-chilling imagery, all announce God's final victory, but – just as with the motif of the kingdom – there is a slight change of direction. The Day of the Lord, we might say, is now here, but not fully here.

It is important to realize that Jesus' ministry has reinterpreted many of the Old Testament hopes, killing off some of the narrow misreading of them that his contemporaries may have held. The Last Days not only usher in the kingdom; they also usher out a raft of other, wrong ideas. There are three stages in God's promise plan, which we might call the *no longer*, the *now*, and the *not yet*. Running the idea of the kingdom, or the Last Days, through the grid in Table 3.2 shows where we now live. It is announcing that we now live in

No longer	Now	Not yet	
Kingdom	The physical restoration of the tribes of Israel in their promised homeland under an earthly king who has defeated their political enemies	The personal acknowledgment of Jesus' Kingship by men and women who turn from their rebellion, accept his pardon, live under his rule and promise, and look for his final victory	The future physical restoration of all races in a new heaven and a new earth, under a heavenly and earthly King who has defeated all their enemies, including death
Last Days	A wholly future event, marked by resurrection, judgment, vindication and punishment	The period in which we live, because Jesus' resurrection was the first of its kind and marked God's vindication of his work on the cross and his inauguration as universal King	The remaining part of the future event, marked by everyone else's resurrection, judgment vindication and punishment

Table 3.2

column 2, and that column 3 is coming, which is what Joel has identified as prophecy, dreams and visions, and which Peter is now
engaged in. The new era we live in makes the next phase more likely
and credible, because the time of judgment is preceded by a time of
gifts which announce that judgment.

But Peter also touches another note that he will close on: everyone
who calls on the name of the Lord will be saved. Who is this Lord?
What is his name? And how can we be saved? At this point, having reset
the clock according to God's new timetable, Peter introduces Jesus.

This Jesus . . . 2:22–24

Peter summarizes three aspects of Jesus' work that would have been familiar to his hearers, if controversial: his life and teaching (v. 22); his death (v. 23); and his resurrection (v. 24). But Peter ties each one to God: Jesus' life and teaching was accredited by God (v. 22); his death was purposed by God (v. 23); and his resurrection was accomplished by God (v. 24). So, although there were present that day both people who had seen Jesus' miracles and heard his teaching and those who had planned and were implicated in his death (notice Peter's careful and accusatory use of 'you', v. 23), and among the believers there were those who had seen the risen Jesus, clearly God was in control. The vindication of Jesus is obviously somehow linked to the passage in Joel.

This Jesus is the Christ: 2:25–32

Peter's mention of the resurrection of Jesus needs fuller explanation, because it was quite clearly an event on a different level from the resurrection of Lazarus or of Jairus' daughter. Taking yet another of the Psalms which describe the suffering and vindication of the King, he gives Jesus the title of God's 'Holy One' (v. 27) and shows how David prophesied that this royal Holy One would not rot in a tomb. So, logically, either King David was talking about himself, in which case he was plain wrong, because his tomb was now a tourist trap (v. 29), or he was talking about someone else, another king. Kings were anointed, or smeared, with oil at their coronation, so it is natural that the title of 'Anointed One' or 'Smeared One' should be applied to them. In Hebrew that title is the word *Messiah*, and in Greek, *Christ*.

If David was dead, he was obviously not the Christ. Peter, however, had met Jesus, who had been raised from the dead. If Psalm 16:8–11 is true, then Peter's argument has proved that Jesus is the Christ.

This Jesus is the Lord: 2:33–35

A second quotation is at the heart of the second answer to this question of Jesus' identity, this time from Ps. 110:1, a verse that Jesus himself used in order to make people think about who he was (Luke 20:42–43). If David was the pre-eminent king, how could he call someone else 'Lord'? That was a title that should have been reserved for God, the Lord, but David has removed that option already, for

The Lord said to my Lord:
  'Sit at my right hand
until I make your enemies
  a footstool for your feet.'

If the Lord is God, who is the other 'my Lord'? Peter's answer is that the fact that Jesus ascended to heaven (and therefore can no longer be seen or heard) is linked to the fact that he has the authority to give the Spirit in the way the crowd can now see and hear. This must be because he shares his Father's throne, for only God can send God's Spirit. If Jesus shares his Father's throne, it is right to call both him and his Father, separately, 'Lord'.

Jesus is therefore Lord and Christ: 2:36

The biblical logic of what Peter has said is quite clear and compelling. Part one is that the Psalms say that the Messiah will be raised; Jesus has been raised; and therefore Jesus is the Messiah. To that the apostles are witnesses (v. 32). Part two is that the Psalms say that there will be another Lord, under God the Lord, who will reign with him; Jesus (as the gift of the Spirit shows) reigns with the Father, and therefore Jesus is the Lord. That is what the crowd have witnessed in what they have seen and heard. Or, as Peter puts it, 'Therefore let all Israel be assured of this: God has made this Jesus . . . both Lord and Christ.'

That is great news. Or, at least, it would be if it were not for the three words we have omitted from v. 36: 'God has made this Jesus *whom you crucified* both Lord and Christ.' That suddenly turns it into the worst version of the event imaginable: they were directly responsible for the murder of God's anointed King, and they did so in full knowledge of his claims. This explains their terror-stricken question, 'Brothers, what shall we do?' Remember what Peter has taught about the Last Day as a Day of Judgment, now moved on a notch because of Jesus' resurrection, and Jesus' unique role as God's vindicated agent who will reign 'until I [God] make your enemies a footstool for your [Jesus'] feet.'

Wonderfully, the answer to their question lies back in the quotation from Joel where Peter began his sermon. 'Everyone who calls on the name of the Lord will be saved' (v. 21). Everything he has explained has been an expansion of the *name* concept. By the wonderful wisdom of God, the one who can save them is the very one they have crucified. Weeks before, they had identified with Jesus' executioners, but the way of rescue now is to be identified with him by being 'baptised . . . in the name of Jesus Christ'; even the sin of knowingly murdering God can be forgiven. And they will even receive the benefit of his victory celebrations, for they too will receive the gift of the Spirit, who will involve them in the new task of taking this great news to those who are as close as their own children, and as remote as those who are far off. It is, once again, a wonderful, all-embracing gospel, which says to those who have crucified their only hope that their only hope is the one they have crucified.

Authentic Christianity: 2:42–47

Luke's little summary of Christian lifestyle in vv. 42–47 is attractive and justifiably famous. The apostles are marked out as being unique in their teaching authority (because they are the only authorized witnesses) and in their capacity to work wonders and miraculous signs, which marked Jesus' ministry (v. 22) as being authenticated by God, and which Joel had said were signs of the Last Days (v. 19). As the church moves out of Jerusalem we shall see how these ripples spread and change as the apostles are no longer available in their authoritative capacity. Luke is quite clear here, though, that what we are witnessing in Jerusalem is more than answered prayers for healing, wonderful as those are; it is God authenticating that this message of forgiveness in the name of the risen, reigning Jesus is true.

The response of the new church to this teaching is growth in the four areas of knowledge ('they devoted themselves to the apostles' teaching'), love ('they devoted themselves to . . . the fellowship'), hospitality ('they devoted themselves to . . . the breaking of bread')[1] and prayer ('they devoted themselves to . . . prayer'). The result was a respect and an attractiveness in their common living that won many to the cause of the gospel, and is a direct challenge to the individualism and materialism in many of our churches.

---

1. Possibly, but not definitely, something based on the Lord's Supper.

4 | The gathering: 3:1 – 6:7

It is at this stage in Acts that a reader can start to be confused; if that reader happens to be a preacher or Bible study leader, then there is room for confusing others. A series of events occurs, but it can be quite hard to discern any order or pattern. Since real life is like that, we might not expect anything else, but the significance of Acts as Scripture and the care with which we have seen the material handled so far ought to lead us to be more cautious in our estimation.

A summary of this section looks like Table 4.1 (overleaf).

Laying out the elements of the section in this way is a good exercise, because of the ability it gives to see over a whole section and to begin to draw some connections which were previously hidden. Four patterns begin to emerge.

It becomes evident that events happen twice

The frequent doubling-up of events becomes obvious as soon as it is seen once. For instance, examine the parallels in Table 4.2. Even when the events are not repeated, there is an obvious overlap between them, as in the two sections on money and stewardship.

3:1 – 4:4	Peter heals a crippled beggar in 'the name of the Lord'	3:1–10
	Peter speaks to the crowd about that healing's meaning:	
	Jesus is God's Servant and Prophet	3:11–26
	Peter and John are arrested	4:1–3
	The consequence of their activity is an increased number	
	of converts	4:4
4:5–22	Peter makes a defence of the gospel at his hearing and	
	has to answer the question 'By what power or what	
	name did you do this?'	4:5–20
	Peter and John are released	4:21–22
4:23–31	The Christians pray for increased boldness despite the threats	
4:32–37	One Christian brings money to the apostles' feet	
5:1–11	Two Christians bring money to the apostles' feet, attempt	
	to deceive the apostles and God, and face the consequences	
5:12–16	The apostles preach, heal and make converts	
5:17–40	The apostles are re-arrested, but are miraculously released	
5:41–42	The apostles preach more boldly	
6:1–6	The apostles appoint the seven to handle the money	
6:7	Summary and conclusion sentence	

Table 4.1

3:1–10	Healing		5:12–16	Healing and preaching
3:11–26	Preaching			
4:1–4	Arrest		5:17–21a	Arrest
4:5–22	Hearing		5:21b–41	Trial
	Testimony			Testimony
	Release			Release
4:23–31	Prayer for more boldness		5:42	Prayer for more boldness
	is answered			is answered
4:32 – 5:11	Money and stewardship		6:1–6	Money and stewardship
			6:7	Conclusion

Table 4.2

That does not mean that this pattern says everything about those sections; the second section on money, for instance, has a major teaching element concerning the role of the apostles as authoritative teachers. Nor does noticing this pattern imply that these events might not have occurred in this way. Luke has carefully ordered his material so that it makes sense to his readers, and 'making sense' means making theological sense, not just chronological sense. Luke means us to notice these patterns, so that we do not lose our way.

The second time events occur, there is growth

Once we become aware of this doubling-up of events, a second pattern becomes visible. Using that same grid, we can notice in Table 4.3 that the second time around there is a significant increase, whether of blessing or opposition.

3:1–10	Healing *Peter (accompanied by John) heals one man*	5:12–16	Healing and preaching *The apostles (plural) heal many*
3:11–26	Preaching *Many believe (4:4)*		*'More and more' believe (5:14)* *Crowds gather (5:16)*
4:1–4	*Peter and John* are arrested	5:17–21a	*The apostles* are arrested *and miraculously released*
4:5–22	*Informal hearing* Testimony Released *with a command* (4:18)	5:21b–41	*Formal trial* Testimony Released *after sentence (5:40)*
4:23–31	Prayer for more boldness is answered	5:42	Prayer for more boldness is answered, *which increases the scope of their ministry (5:42)*
4:32 – 5:11	Money and stewardship *Barnabas, Ananias and Sapphira bring money to the apostles' feet*	6:1–6	Money and stewardship *The apostles delegate the increasing workload to the Seven*
		6:7	Conclusion

Table 4.3

The care with which all this is assembled argues that Luke is in charge of his material to make his points. He has shown increase in the number of healings (confirming the continuing link with Jesus and the biblical significance of the apostles); the opportunity and clarity of evangelistic preaching (which will be looked at below); the number of converts; the experience of suffering; the courageous resilience; and the demarcation between Israel and the church, as teaching provokes opposition, which in turn raises the cost of loyal discipleship, and the reality of the truth of Christianity. If what the apostles say is true, then some of their hearers are to blame for the death of the Messiah (5:28), and those who treat them lightly are despising God (5:9). By the same token, the blessings that follow the gospel are not illusory either.

This section has a unique emphasis on the Old Testament

The Old Testament is quoted throughout Acts, of course, but the explicit references and less obvious echoes are such a motif of this panel in Acts that Luke must intend something by it. Once again, the chart in Table 4.4 will prove a useful summary.

3:1–10	Healing		
3:11–26	Preaching	5:12–16	Healing and preaching

3:13	The God of Abraham, Isaac and Jacob, the God of our fathers (Exod. 3:6, burning bush)	5:12	Miraculous signs and wonders. These words are used repeatedly, with variations, of God's
3:13	Servant (Isa. 52:13)		saving acts at the
3:14	Holy one – Elisha (2 Kgs 4:9), Aaron (Ps. 106:16) Righteous one (Isa. 53:11)		Exodus (e.g. Deut. 4:34). This puts the events of Acts on the same level as those great and unique
3:18	All the prophets		events of the past.

3:21	The holy prophets	
3:22–23	(Deut. 18:15–19, Lev. 23:29), and Samuel (no ref.)	
3:24	All the prophets from Samuel on	
3:25	Heirs of the prophets and heirs of the covenant (Gen. 12:3)	

4:1–4	Peter and John are arrested	5:17–21	The apostles are arrested and miraculously released
		5:19	The angel of the Lord (e.g. Exod. 3:2)
4:5–22	Informal hearing Testimony Released	5:22–41	Formal trial Testimony Released
4:11	The stone (Ps. 118:22, but also Isa. 28:16 and Zech. 10:4)	5:30	Tree (Deut. 21:22–23) God of our fathers (Exod. 3:6: see on 3:13 above)
4:23–31	Prayer for more boldness is answered	5:42	Prayer for more boldness is answered
4:25–26	Ps. 2:1–2		
4:31	Exod. 19:18 (Sinai)		
4:32 – 5:11	Money and stewardship	6:1–6	Money and stewardship
4:34	Joshua 7:1 – Achan	6:1–6	Jethro and Moses (Exod. 18) Laying hands (Num. 27:15–23, on Joshua)
5:2	'kept back' money from God		
5:9–11	Exod. 17:2; Deut. 6:16 – 'test the Lord'		
5:11	Assembly (church) (Deut. 4:10; 9:10; 10:4; 18:16)		
		6:7	Conclusion

Table 4.4

Those references confirm two main themes in this section.

The authentic Messiah is the suffering Messiah, as the Old Testament foretold

The shock of the centrality of the death and resurrection of Jesus runs through this section. His death is shocking because of the common expectation that the Messiah would be glorious, and his resurrection is shocking because it means that humans still have to deal with him as their Lord and Judge. Both the cross and the resurrection will be good and bad news, depending on the response of the hearers. But Luke is insistent that this pattern of suffering, death and resurrection, is the one God had planned all the way through, as his numerous references to Old Testament teaching about Jesus' death will show.

The Christian believers are the continuation of the people of God

The apostles are appointed by God to be his designated messengers, in a way that seems especially to echo the role of Moses at Sinai and in the desert. The people of God, then, are those who believe the apostles: who cluster around their teaching and obey it, as the Israelites had camped around first the mountain of God and then the tabernacle.

This emphasis in fulfilment might help to answer some of the inevitable questions that come up in Acts. Are the deaths of Ananias and Sapphira, for instance, something that God intends to happen in all churches after this, or are they a one-off warning to bring our attention to the fact that he has not changed? The parallel with the Wanderings in the Desert might help us to see the significance of the event, and the fact that it occurs in this section of Acts, with its unique fulfilment theology, might show that a warning is more likely than a precedent (see above, p. 33).

This section shows us the gospel

This unit of Acts contains three evangelistic sermons from Peter: in 3:12–26, 4:8–12 and 5:30–32. Once again, laying them out together in Table 4.5 shows us the core of the gospel message.

The facts	You killed him God raised him We saw him	3:13–15	4:10–11	5:30, 32
The offer	Forgiveness and the Holy Spirit	3:16–19		
The reason	The return of Christ	3:20–23	4:12	5:31–32
The response	Repentance and faith	3:24–26		

Table 4.5

Comparing the three sermons like this also shows a critical part of Luke's writing strategy that we need to grasp early on. When Luke reproduces sermons that repeat earlier material, he condenses down the material that is simply identical in shape, and expands only material that is new. So we should not imagine that Peter was here preaching successively shorter sermons, but that Luke is telling us that he was preaching substantially the same sermon. Here, then, is the core of the gospel message as it was preached to Jews in Jerusalem. It will become clear as we move on that Luke uses this condensation technique with great effect as he shows how the gospel spreads to Jews and Gentiles who know little, if anything, about Jesus, and (in the case of some of the Gentiles) hardly anything about God at all.

5 | Beyond the land: 6:8 – 9:31

Introduction

This section has three main characters – Stephen, Philip and Saul – and they are the key to the way the story unlocks. Stephen and Philip have already been introduced as the first two in the list of deacons (6:5), so it is a shock to encounter them in this section as evangelists and preachers. Since the deacons were appointed to 'serve tables' while the apostles were appointed to 'the ministry [literally, 'the service'] of the word', we might expect it to be the apostles whom we find preaching. But Luke has an understanding that everyone is to be involved in the task of spreading the message; hence he deliberately puts at centre stage in evangelism those whom we might think he has disqualified. The apostles may have their unique rôle, and Stephen and Philip may be employed in a particular way to release them from that, but the apostles' delegating administration to Stephen and Philip does not mean that Stephen and Philip can delegate evangelism to the apostles.

Stephen has the first main section here, from 6:8 to 8:3, which includes a long sermon and his stoning to death. Philip comes

second, from 8:4 to 8:40, and he evangelizes in Samaria and its surrounding area. He is present at the odd scene where the first
Samaritans believe and are baptized, but do not receive the Holy
Spirit until two of the apostles arrive (8:14–17). Saul's conversion and
commissioning to be an apostle run from 9:1–30, although Luke has
already introduced him as consenting to Stephen's death in 7:58 and
8:1. To the first-time reader, of course, Saul is merely one more character in the cast list; he is not revealed to be the famous Paul until
13:9. Luke gives the next concluding verse in 9:31.

So here are three characters with three different kinds of story: a
trial scene with a sermon before an execution; a couple of snapshots
of one man's ministry; and a conversion and commissioning. Luke
has constructed three key motifs which run through them and hold
them together.

Geography

Inevitably with Acts, once Luke starts to move outside Jerusalem into
the next area for work the reader wants to consult a map. And that is
entirely right. We need to see that the story starts with Stephen in
Jerusalem, but because of the persecution that follows his death the
church was scattered throughout Judea and Samaria. Several things
call for our attention here.

The first is that Luke makes clear that the people who were scattered comprised everyone 'except the apostles' (8:1) and that those
people immediately went about 'preaching the word' (8:4). Once
again, even though the apostles had a unique rôle, every believer had
a responsibility to teach the message.

Secondly, we should not miss the significance of the phrase 'Judea
and Samaria' (8:1). In 1:8 Jesus told the church that the second phase
of their work would come when they moved out of Jerusalem into
the two halves of the old divided kingdom of Israel, and in this
section it begins to happen. Jesus is rebuilding the monarchy of
David, but in a radically different way. So although we need a map to
see where Judea and Samaria were, we need to read the map biblically, for on its own it will tell us nothing but grid references. Perhaps
the apostles had imagined that the move outwards would happen as
they planned, strategized and sent task forces, but it actually occurs
under the whip of persecution. Incidentally, that persecution was

orchestrated by Saul; Luke is underlining how deeply unlikely it was that he should be converted (8:3–4).

The third geographical note is that the first part of Philip's ministry in Samaria, as we watch the rebuilding of the Judea–Samaria kingdom in close-up, requires two apostles to travel from Jerusalem to Samaria and back again. Clearly the ties with the old city are strong; they are theological as well as personal, for what Philip is doing needs approval. That approval, once given, does not need to be repeated, though: the next story involves a man travelling away from Jerusalem into Ethiopia, who is converted and baptized without any Jerusalem contact. The cutting of the cord with Jerusalem, so that the churches are equal without one being prime – not dependent but interdependent – is a little subplot of Acts.

Fourthly, Saul's story is also framed by geographical markers, for he travels from Jerusalem to Damascus as a persecutor, but reverses his journey as an evangelist.

Who can be saved?

Geography is never on its own in Acts, because the story concerns people being saved, and the map references are giving us clues to a deeper question about the reach of the gospel and the make-up of the church. The conversions in Jerusalem teach that Jews may believe in the Lord Jesus. This section tells us that, racially, Samaritans and ultimately Gentiles may believe and be saved (9:15). Luke puts the focus on one man, Saul, and shows that even someone who is violently opposed to Christianity may be converted. As we shall see, it would be a mistake to see Saul's conversion as a model conversion, for not everyone is that hostile to Christianity from the outset, and no-one since Paul has been commissioned as an apostle. Nevertheless, it is a model in some senses, not least here of the extent of God's grace. That is how Paul uses his conversion story in 1 Timothy 1:16.

Trouble

Life becomes deeply unpleasant and dangerous for the Christians in this section, who not only have to give up their homes and work, but also see the first believer killed simply for being a believer. In Luke's typical way, then, Stephen's death is presented as one instance of a much wider pressure on the church, whose members seem to have stayed faithful under the ultimate pressure.

In God's sovereign plans, of course, the pressure on the Christians to leave Jerusalem actually means that more people hear the message. This pattern of trouble leading to teaching is recurrent in Acts. It is not the only pattern of evangelistic work we see, and Paul clearly operated with a deliberate strategy for church planting and nurturing, but it is sufficiently frequent to be a major theme. As Jesus says about Saul in this section, 'This man is my chosen instrument to carry my name before the Gentiles and their kings, and before the people of Israel. I will show him how much he must suffer for my name' (9:15–16).

With those three themes in place, we can turn to each main character individually.

a. Stephen: 6:8 – 8:3

The key to grasping the heart of Stephen's message is to understand the charge laid against him. In 6:11 the plotters name it as 'words of blasphemy against Moses [that is, against the law and the traditions protecting it] and against God'. In 6:13 the false witnesses allege, 'This fellow never stops speaking against this holy place [that is, the temple] and against the law.' And their evidence in 6:14 is that 'We have heard him say that this Jesus of Nazareth will destroy this place and change the customs Moses handed down to us.' So the blasphemy has either two or three charges: one is 'Moses . . . the law . . . Moses', a second is 'God', and a third is 'this holy place . . . this place'. Since the patterns and pairing are so close, it seems worth combining the second and third charges and understanding the attack on the temple to be an attack on God, as it was his dwelling place. We would expect, then, for this message to address the double charge of blasphemy against the law and the temple.

Before that happens, there is an extended synopsis of Genesis 12 through to Exodus 18 (7:2–36). Some have thought this section to show Stephen as rambling, or even impertinent in trying to teach the theologically educated Sanhedrin. But, read attentively, the sermon shows that Stephen is not merely repeating the history, but sounding a consistent note throughout – the note of theological geography.

First, he introduces three principal players to establish a point – again, a chart will help. (See Table 5.1.) Once again, the aim is not an exhaustive commentary but an attempt to see the main highway running through the text.

Abraham	7:2–8	
	Where did God appear to Abraham?	Mesopotamia
	Where did Abraham settle?	Haran
	What part of the promised land did Abraham own?	The promise
Joseph	7:9–15	
	Where was God with Joseph?	In Egypt – repeated *six times* in the text
	Where did Jacob, Joseph's father, die?	In Egypt
	Where did the rest of the family go to?	Egypt
Moses	7:17–36	
	Where did Moses grow up?	Egypt
	Where did Moses flee to?	Midian
	Where did God appear to Moses?	Sinai, in the desert
	Where did God send Moses?	Egypt
	Where did God call the people to go to?	Sinai, in the desert

Table 5.1

By the account up to verse 36, Stephen has made a repeated and quite critical point for the development of the story, for it appears that all of God's principal dealings in establishing his covenant lay outside the promised land. God, then, is not tied to any geographical location. That may seem obvious, but it needed to be established before Stephen could move on to his principal issues, the law and the temple.

Continuing with Table 5.2 and the time of Moses, Stephen addresses first the *law* (37–43) and then the *temple*, under the theme of its predecessor the tabernacle (44–50).

Moses and the law 7:37–43	
Where did Israel receive the law?	'In the assembly in the desert' (Sinai, Midian)
Moses and the tabernacle 7:44–50	
Where did Israel have the tabernacle?	'In the desert' (Sinai, Midian)

Table 5.2

Not only was the covenant not inaugurated in the Land (though it promised the Land as a means to bless the Gentiles); neither the law nor the tabernacle was tied to the physical land of Israel. What, though, was the response of the people to these two great gifts? Table 5.3 explains.

Israel and the law	
What was Israel's original response to the law?	7:39 They refused to obey it
What was Israel's contemporary response to the law?	7:53 'you . . . have not obeyed it'
The charge against Stephen	'He speaks against the law'
Stephen's response	'You do not keep the law'
Israel and the tabernacle	
What did Israel know about the tabernacle / temple?	God does not dwell in houses or temples (7:49–50)
What did Israel do with that knowledge?	Idolized the temple and the land as 'this holy place' (6:13)
The charge against Stephen	'He speaks against the temple'
Stephen's response	'You idolize the temple'

Table 5.3

In summary, so far:

- All of God's major covenant dealings occurred outside the promised land.
- The law was given outside the land.
- The tabernacle was given outside the land.
- The typical Old Testament reaction to the law was to break it – and Stephen's hearers do that.
- The typical Old Testament reaction to the Temple was to idolize it – and Stephen's hearers do that.

And here comes the critical turning point:

- The typical Old Testament reaction to the prophets who pointed those sins out was to kill them (7:52a).
- The typical Old Testament reaction to the prophets who prophesied the Messiah was to kill them (7:52b).
- And now you have completed that reaction by killing the Messiah (6:53).

It is not surprising that their response in v. 54 is fury. But that, of course, merely proves Stephen's point, for their reaction to *him* is precisely the same reaction that Jesus and all the line of prophets before him experienced. The purpose of the law and the tabernacle and temple was to point out and provide for our human rebellion, and their reaction to these purposes was sinful and rebellious. So Stephen has turned the tables: rather than prove himself innocent, he has proved his accusers guilty. At their anger, Stephen looks up to heaven, and sees God's glory, and Jesus enthroned. Notice that this was not a vision at his martyrdom, but a justification by Jesus at what he had just said, for once again God's great dealings with people lie outside the land and are now located with the risen and reigning Jesus. The gospel here, once again, is 'You killed him; God raised him; I [Stephen] saw him.'

It is a magnificent and theologically rich sermon, which has occurred at precisely the right moment for the unfolding narrative, for Stephen has provided the biblical justification for moving outside the physical city of Jerusalem, with its temple and law, and into the world of the Gentiles. Or, to qualify that in the light of Stephen's message, the temple and the law, correctly understood, have always taught that God's plan is global, not limited to one land, and that the gospel was always intended to reach all nations, not one. The first Jewish Christian to tell a non-Jew about salvation in Jesus was courageous, but thoroughly biblical.

To notice how careful and subtle a writer Luke is, by the way, think again of the significance of the word 'church' as it appeared for the first time, after the death of Ananias and Sapphira. There we saw how it transferred the titles and awesome reality of being the people of God onto the fledgling Christians. Buried in Stephen's speech is another reference to the people of God, this time as 'the assembly in the desert' (7:38) who were given the law. The word commonly translated 'assembly' here is the word usually translated 'church': *ekklēsia*. In other words, God's people, given God's words and assured of his presence outside the land, were called the church. And what is the next step of the story to which Luke will turn?

> On that day a great persecution broke out against the church at Jerusalem, and all except the apostles were scattered. Godly men buried Stephen and mourned deeply for him. But Saul began to destroy the church.
>
> (8:1-3)

The gospel is once again about to be outside the land, and the next part of this panel tells us how it spread.

b. Philip: 8:4-40

Samaria

As we saw in chapter 2 (pp. 33-35), Philip is the man who typifies the church moving into Judea and Samaria and taking the gospel with it. The Samaritans were regarded with deep disapproval by the Jews of the day, which is why Jesus caused scandal by talking about a *Good* Samaritan (Luke 10:25-37). The history of the Samaritans can be difficult to plumb, but it seems that they function here, theologically and geographically, as those who were separated from authentic Judah: the descendants of the rebellion of Jeroboam against Rehoboam, and who set up a second monarchy (1 Kgs 12). Whatever the physical lineage of the contemporary inhabitants of Samaria, the fact that Luke consistently twins Judea and Samaria (1:8, 8:1 and 9:31, the concluding verse to our section) makes it likely, in my view, that he has them in his mind as those who were racially mixed, who were Jewish in part, but rejected the temple and the monarchy. 'Semi-detached Jews' might be a mild way of describing their status. This, then, is the first theological and racial hurdle the gospel must cross, and it must cross it precisely because of Jesus' command in 1:8.

So Philip preached in Samaria, and preached the same message as was heard in Jerusalem, that Jesus is the *Christ*, Messiah. The last time that title was used in Acts it served as a summary sentence of the entire Christian message: 'Day after day, in the temple courts and from house to house, they never stopped teaching and proclaiming the good news that Jesus is the Christ' (5:42). By using it as the summary of Philip's message here, Luke is indicating it was the same message, with the same results: some wonderful, like the 'miraculous signs', exorcisms, 'great joy' and baptisms, and one in particular troubling, in the response of a man named Simon. Simon, who was nicknamed 'Great Power' because it was said he had 'divine power' (8:10), became fascinated by the miracles that he saw accompanying Philip.

Before we understand the puzzle that is Simon, however, we need to understand the puzzle of the apostles. They heard in Jerusalem of what was happening in Samaria and sent Peter and John. The puzzle here is to see why they were sent. Could it be because Philip's message was defective? Hardly – Luke has taken pains to show that this was the authentic message with the authentic responses. Could it be because his ministry was defective? Again it seems unlikely, because Luke has pointed out that there was an authentic response of people believing and being baptized (8:12). But somehow, for some reason, the Samaritans had not received the Holy Spirit, and this is why the apostles travelled. Here we need to keep the theological programme of Acts clear and remember just how significant – theologically significant – this division between Jew and Samaritan really is. If God had sent the Spirit on the believers in Samaria without any comment, they would have continued on with the division still existing between Jew and semi-Jew. This delay in giving the

Spirit forced the apostles to authenticate this as a true work of God, and therefore that Samaritans can become believers on an equal standing with Jews. It is a breathtaking moment, as the gospel comes face to face with potential racial division for the first time and forces the division to give way. Race is no barrier to hearing the gospel of God; hence the Samaritans experience an echo of Pentecost (8:14–17).

It is critical that we see what is going on here, for otherwise we would expect this to occur times without number, each time a new people group is reached. Luke insists, though, that this is a single, programmatic event to validate not just that *these* people can be reached, but that therefore *any* people in this situation can be reached, and he reinforces it with the story of the Ethiopian. The gateway to the Samaritans had been officially opened, and so Peter and John 'returned to Jerusalem, preaching the gospel in many Samaritan villages' (8:25).

So why is the story of Simon the Great One here? Notice the words that come up through the account: 'sorcery . . . amazed . . . boasted . . . great . . . divine power . . . Great Power . . . amazed . . . ' This man has Samaria dazzled by his magic. And when Philip appeared performing 'signs' that 'astonished' even Simon, there was bound to be a clash of understandings and values. Simon seemed to understand and even believe the gospel, but the reality of the apostles' giving of the Spirit he saw as a trick or technique that could be learnt and mastered. He wanted, then, to have power over the Spirit: to control him and even sell him. The first temptation that the Christians faced, as they moved into Samaritan territory, was to distort the gospel to be about power, and to preach Jesus not as the crucified one but as a means to powerful results. Just as in Jerusalem, the scandal was the cross. That becomes clearer in the second, contrasting picture.

Ethiopia

It is hard to say what the exact spiritual status of this man was: God-fearer; proselyte; Diaspora Jew? Had he heard the apostles preach in Jerusalem, or had he missed them in his worship at the temple? We do know he was an Ethiopian, and therefore black, and that he was a eunuch. Both factors are hugely significant.

Eunuchs were debarred from being priests in the temple (Lev. 21:17–20) or from being part of the assembly in the temple (Deut.

23:1). In other words, this man was returning from a trip to the temple which would have physically reinforced for him that he was not a fully participant member of God's people. Similarly, as a foreigner he (like most of us) had at best a welcomed but second-level status in God's people (e.g. Deut. 14:21; 15:3). So this man had pressed as close as he could to entering the temple, the symbol of God's presence and mercy, but was banned. He, like the Samaritans, was – at best – semi-detached from Israel.

Stephen's sermon, though, had told a different story, for the tabernacle was located outside the land, when all of God's people were strangers and foreigners. And here Luke shows us that there is good news for foreigners too.

The man was reading Isaiah 53. Philip explained that Jesus is that Messiah Isaiah foretold (8:35); the man believed (8:36), was baptized (8:38) and rejoiced (8:39). In other words, *exactly the same sequence of events as occurred in Samaria* happened here in the desert – with one major exception. Peter and John did not turn up to lay hands on him, because Pentecost does not have to be duplicated every time someone semi-detached from Israel is converted; just the first time. That is the reason these two stories are stapled together: Luke shows it was physically impossible for the Ethiopian to have any contact with the apostles at all after his conversion, yet he received the Spirit every bit as fully as did the Samaritans. As do we.

Samaria and Ethiopia

It would be so much easier for our evangelistic efforts if every non-Christian we met happened to be reading Isaiah 53 on the train, but of course that is not Luke's point here, and it should not shape our expectations. He has a theological and structural reason for emphasizing this passage. What marks out the Suffering Servant of Isaiah is precisely his suffering: 'led . . . slaughter . . . silent . . . humiliation . . . his life was taken' (Acts 8:32–33). It is a marked contrast to the list which typified Simon Magus: 'sorcery . . . amazed . . . boasted . . . great . . . divine power . . . Great Power . . . amazed' (8:9–11). This is surely the point: where Simon is marked by greatness and power, Jesus is marked by humiliation and suffering. What is the gospel that goes out from Jerusalem? The suffering Messiah. What is the danger Christians meet in Samaria? The attraction of power.

One final observation bears noticing. The climax of those Servant Songs in Isaiah includes promises that resonate so much for this story that it is almost impossible to think that Luke did not want us to read them through to the end: themes of foreigners worshipping at the temple and eunuchs being fruitful abound. Here is Isaiah 56:3–8:

> Let no foreigner who has bound himself to the LORD say,
> 'The LORD will surely exclude me from his people.'
> And let not any eunuch complain,
> 'I am only a dry tree.'
>
> For this is what the LORD says:
>
> 'To the eunuchs who keep my Sabbaths,
> who choose what pleases me
> and hold fast to my covenant –
> to them I will give within my temple and its walls
> a memorial and a name
> better than sons and daughters;
> I will give them an everlasting name
> that will not be cut off.
> And foreigners who bind themselves to the LORD
> to serve him,
> to love the name of the LORD,
> and to worship him,
> all who keep the Sabbath without desecrating it
> and who hold fast to my covenant –
> these I will bring to my holy mountain
> and give them joy in my house of prayer.
> Their burnt offerings and sacrifices
> will be accepted on my altar;
> for my house will be called
> a house of prayer for all nations.'
> The Sovereign LORD declares –
> he who gathers the exiles of Israel:
> 'I will gather still others to them
> besides those already gathered.'

c. Saul: 9:1–30

Luke has already alerted his readers to Saul's significance: he approved of Stephen's death and indirectly caused Philip's ministry (8:1). Now, though, Saul has a crucial part in the story. Luke shows that it is crucial by both the length he gives it here and the fact that it is repeated twice, with minor variations of theme, later in the book.

Four structural elements are worth noting, to help us understand and teach this familiar story today.

The authority of Jesus

Saul's conversion is to a gospel of unmistakable authority. Notice how Saul calls him 'Lord' (v. 5), and how Luke repeats the emphasis when 'the Lord' speaks to Ananias (v. 10) and he replies 'Yes, Lord'; then 'the Lord' speaks again (v. 11) and Ananias again answers, 'Lord' (v. 13). 'The Lord' speaks a third time in verse 15, and Ananias tells Saul that 'the Lord' has sent him. From the beginning of the chapter Luke has been heading towards this confrontation: Saul was 'breathing out murderous threats against the Lord's disciples'. It is a relatively frequent title in Acts, but it is unmissable here. Whatever had happened in his thinking prior to this moment, and he himself indicated later that Jesus had been troubling him for some time (26:14), this single event revolutionized his entire life as he realized that Jesus is *Lord*. He travelled to Damascus to take disciples, and left as a disciple maker. He arrived to take prisoners, and left as a fugitive from the forces he had until recently led. In the sense that he recognized Jesus' authority, his conversion is a model for any conversion.

The commissioning of Saul

Yet his conversion is an unrepeatable occurrence because it involved a heavenly commissioning, which Paul later related as the moment when he was called to be an apostle (1 Cor. 15:3–11). So it would be a mistake to read this as a merely heavenly vision of who Jesus is, although that would be true. Rather, this is a resurrection appearance of Jesus, which was needed to make Paul a genuine apostle and witness of the resurrection – the last resurrection appearance. Saul appears to have taken this straight to heart, for his preaching from the outset involved the present role of Jesus, who 'is the Son of God' (9:20) and 'is the Christ' (9:22).

The next stage

Saul's commissioning was to the next stage of the gospel outreach, to the Gentiles and the rulers (v. 15), and this becomes the main plot of the second half of Acts. It is tempting to think that his conversion was necessary because it proves that if God can convert him he can convert anyone, which is true. But we know from Paul's letters that his status as a real apostle was constantly challenged, and there is something appealing in the idea that Paul was 'grafted in' to the company of the Apostles just as the Gentiles, his mission field, were 'grafted in' to Israel (Rom. 11:17–24).

Hardship

Jesus makes clear from the outset that suffering for the gospel will be integral to Saul's ministry (v. 16). That is, not only will he have to suffer because he will preach a message that offends, but that it is right that he suffers in this way. Just as Jesus is persecuted when the church is persecuted (9:4), so Paul will suffer because his master suffered. So Saul's conversion may be unique and the Samaritans' conversion may be unique, but Stephen's suffering was normative. The Ethiopian, whose conversion was the normative one in this section, taught that from Isaiah 53.

Coordinating themes

Taking the overarching view of this section, seven features emerge which hold it together and drive the story forwards. These seven are important for understanding the whole, so that any individual part is correctly oriented.

1. *Geography*

Once again Luke gives constant geographical markers. The section starts at the coast at Lydda and Joppa; Cornelius sends from Caesarea to Joppa, and Peter travels from Joppa to Caesarea. Peter then travels from Caesarea to Jerusalem. In a geographically separate (although theologically linked) story, the church at Antioch is seeing the gospel bear fruit, and that church has active links with the Jerusalem church. In Jerusalem, Peter is arrested by Herod, miraculously released, and he leaves. In Caesarea, meanwhile, Herod dies under God's judgment.

The spreading out of the church from Jerusalem is showing both that the churches elsewhere are being solidly established and that the ties with the Jerusalem church are much more those between equals.

Some of the central themes of this section emerge in marked distinction to the Jerusalem church, and Antioch emerges as a new centre for gospel ministry.

2. Race

It is impossible to talk about this section of Acts as if geography were the only marker, because the critical issue is one of nationality. In particular, Acts, in common with the rest of Scripture, divides humankind into two subsets: Jew and Gentile. They are not independent subsets, for the beginning of the division also echoes its final ending too, when God promised Abram:

> I will make you into a great nation
>   and I will bless you;
> I will make your name great,
>   and you will be a blessing.
> I will bless those who bless you,
>   and whoever curses you I will curse;
> and all peoples on earth
>   will be blessed through you.
>   (Gen. 12:2–3)

One of the functions of God-blessed Israel, then, is to be the means by which the Gentiles are blessed, and these chapters show one aspect of how this came about.

It has become standard practice in theological circles to talk of the Bible's overarching pattern as 'salvation history'. Although in the hands of some, that can mean that it is not real history, but functions as a convenient explanatory tool, or myth, it is possible to use it in a more positive way to mean the way in which God has worked in history to bring salvation about. Alongside 'salvation history', though, Luke teaches us two more biblical disciplines: 'salvation geography', as the whole world is brought under the reign of Christ at God's right hand,[1]

---

1. I am grateful to my colleague Dr Matthew Sleeman for the penetrating insight that the physical location of the ascended Jesus relativizes all other physical locations.

and 'salvation ethnography', as we see how God overcomes all racial barriers in the inclusive nature of the gospel.

These are explosive themes in our political climate, and some of Luke's comments might seem to run the risk of anti-Semitism. As we shall see, though, it is the inclusion of both Jew *and* Gentile in the new phenomenon called Christianity that is so startling. It is probably too much to claim as a programmatic statement that Acts as a whole shows churches being deliberately planted to include both Jews and Gentiles, for that would assume that the absence of either group would render a church invalid. It is, however, obviously the case that the early churches would long for evangelism among both groups to be continuous and prayerfully active, and that the healing of that fundamental divide in active church fellowship is totemic of all other divisions being healed as well.

3. The stories
There are two principal plots. The first involves Peter and Cornelius, the key events of which are so critical that they are told at length three times: as they happen; when Peter and Cornelius met and exchanged stories; and when Peter travelled to Jerusalem to recount the event. The second plot involves Peter and Herod, and again is told at length. This divides this section neatly into two large subsections: Peter and Cornelius running from 9:32 to 11:18, and Peter and Herod running from 12:1 to 12:23, with 12:24 as a summary verse.

In between lies the brief snapshot of the church in Antioch (11:19–30), which serves to keep the plot moving forwards and also to counterpoint the main two stories. We are reminded of the church spreading through the persecution following Stephen's death, and of the role of Barnabas and Saul (who has yet to be unveiled as Paul, remember), and we are shown many Gentiles coming to faith, Peter's first story having shown just one in Cornelius. Luke has carefully plotted his sections and is fully in control of his material.

4. Supernaturalism
This section is marked by a series of miraculous events: Aeneas is healed, Dorcas is raised from the dead, Peter has a vision and Cornelius sees an angel (both recounted three times); at Antioch Agabus exercises his ministry as a prophet; in Jerusalem Peter is

miraculously released from prison by the action of an angel; and in
Caesarea Herod dies a horrible death, again at the hands of an angel.

Simultaneously, Luke underlines that these were not everyday
occurrences in the life of the early church. Aeneas was healed, but
before that he had been bedridden, and presumably prayed for, for
eight years. Perhaps it had to be an apostle – or perhaps, in this section
supremely, it had to be Peter – who healed him. Similarly Dorcas had
been sick, and presumably been prayed for, and had died, and possibly
been prayed for again, but it is Peter who becomes the agent of the
needed miracle. Note again Luke's technique of building tension: can
God heal a seriously sick person through Peter? Yes, he can. So can he
raise a definitely dead person through Peter? Again, yes.

The context for Peter's miraculous release from prison was that
James had also been arrested and imprisoned; presumably he too had
been prayed for, but, far from being delivered, he was executed (12:2).
The Christians must have gathered to pray for Peter with considerable anxiety for his safety, and with good cause.

We therefore need to exercise some care here. There is no excuse
for wilful anti-supernaturalism, which tries to explain away the
miraculous as an ordinary event, understood in a particular way. No,
these are all sovereign and miraculous acts of God. But equally there
is no excuse for what we might call 'super-supernaturalism', which
ignores Luke's careful counterpointing of downbeat events with the
splendid. These were not everyday miracles – that is what makes
them so special; God was attesting a stunning and critical move forwards in gospel growth.

5. The message

In this section Peter preaches another evangelistic sermon, the fifth
of his that Luke has recorded so far. Three structural observations
are worth making about it:

- It is almost exactly the same as the previous four that Peter has
  preached.
- It is the first sermon preached to a Gentile. The duplication is not
  Luke being lazy or unobservant, but his careful way of noting that
  as the gospel goes to the Gentiles for the first time, it is precisely the
  same message that is told. This seems to be so overwhelmingly the

case here that we have to assume the Ethiopian eunuch to have had a different spiritual status from Cornelius, for all Cornelius' good works (10:2).

Therefore the Gentiles receive the same gospel as the Jews. There were subtle differences of course: Peter could not say to Cornelius, as he had in Jerusalem on the previous occasions, 'you killed' Jesus (2:23; 3:15; 4:10; 5:30), so he says 'they killed him', and Luke shows Peter giving more of the life-story of Jesus than was needed on previous occasions. But the gospel outline (they killed him; God raised him; we saw him) remains intact, and the gospel offer (forgiveness from judgment; and the gift of the Holy Spirit) is held out in the same way (10:34–43). To put that last point more cautiously: since the gift of the Spirit is God's work, and since the man was a Gentile, Peter does not mention the Spirit. That God gives his Spirit is the critical climax of the story.

• The consequences of the sermon are the same as for the first Jewish Christians and the first Samaritan Christians: a Pentecost, or rather a second echo of Pentecost, to affirm the Gentile inclusion in the great plan of God. The Spirit comes, and the converts speak in tongues.

We should notice again the care with which Luke teaches us through his narrative. Just as the Samaritan story was followed by the Ethiopian's story *without the Pentecost echo* to show what parts of the story are unique and what are universal, so here Cornelius' conversion is followed by the story of the Antiochene Gentiles *again without the Pentecost echo*, to teach us in the same way. Once again, we must be careful to avoid both anti-supernaturalism and super-supernaturalism. Luke is deliberately teaching us that this is a one-off salvation event. Other conversion stories today *may* be accompanied by such visible and audible gifts of the Spirit, but we seriously misread Luke if we think that they must or ought to be. Since everyone on the planet is either Jew or Gentile, every people group on earth has been included in Pentecost.

6. Antioch

In this section Antioch emerges clearly as a new centre for Christian work and ministry. In fact, Luke carefully notes that this is where

Christians were first nicknamed 'Christians' (11:26). There is a sense of completion about the story, now that the gospel has reached the Gentiles and found a home there. Not that this church was a Gentile phenomenon; Luke carefully shows that it was a Jewish–Gentile church, and it was this phenomenon, which transcended the deepest division in humanity, which needed a new name. So Antioch is both the centre of the Gentile mission and the centre of the collection to send relief to the church in Jerusalem. The home that the gospel has found in Antioch is not a Gentile church, but one in which both Jews and Gentiles honour the Lord Jesus.

7. Paul

Marking the complex relationship between Antioch and Jerusalem, Paul emerges as the new focus for Acts. Luke has been tantalizing his readers with Saul, because he wanted to focus on Peter while keeping our interest on the next step as well. These last two points – the emergence of Antioch and the emergence of Paul – are a preparation for the ongoing story: Antioch stepping into the limelight and Jerusalem receding, and Paul becoming the principal human actor.

Narrative flow

With those seven features in place, the narrative sense of the section hangs together well.

Lydda and Joppa: 9:32–43

These two miracles, one of healing and one of resurrection, both occur among and for Christians ('the saints' [9:32], 'disciple' [9:36]), but to keep the clarity of the section we should note that they are *Jewish* Christians. The story of Cornelius loses its sharp focus without that thought. Why are they here? Because the gospel has travelled to the outer limits of Diaspora Judaism, Joppa being on the coast, and Peter has witnessed that. Luke had previously shown Jesus telling a man to get up and walk (Luke 5:17–26) and raising the dead (Luke 8:40–56), and Peter has repeated those miracles here. So, in a way, Peter is at the outer limits of where the gospel had gone, symbolically and theologically at least, and the question arises: what next? The answer lies in the vision of the sheet.

Caesarea and Joppa: 10:1 – 11:18

Peter's vision is so critical that not only does Luke repeat it three times, but the vision itself on the rooftop in Joppa happens three identical times (10:16), each concluding with the words 'Do not call anything impure that God has made clean' (10:15). This moment's importance in the story is compounded by the coordinated visit of the angel to Cornelius. All of which is to tell Peter deliberately to cross over the boundary and knowingly tell the gospel to a Gentile. The story is sometimes referred to not as 'The Conversion of Cornelius', which of course it is, but as 'The Conversion of Peter', which is also a true insight.

This is the massive theological centre of the section, and Peter acknowledged, 'I now realise how true it is that God does not show favouritism but accepts [those] from every nation who fear him and do what is right' (10:34–35). His understanding, of course, was not universalism, in the sense that everyone *will* be saved, but truly global, in the sense that everyone now *may* be saved. So, when the Jerusalem church heard of this, Peter travelled there to confirm that Pentecost had had its final, theologically significant echo.

This episode does raise the question of whether it is plausible that Peter would have taken so long to realize the global nature of the gospel, especially as Jesus had made it explicit that that was what should happen (Luke 24:47, Acts 1:8), but every indication is that what we find obvious many of the first Christians found impossibly difficult to grasp and revolutionary in its impact. On the other hand, however, we find it hard to grasp what they found obvious: namely, that evangelism to those who are Jewish is a task of primary importance, not to be left to a few, and not to be ignored because their faith is monotheistic enough.

Antioch and Jerusalem: 11:19–30

It is critical for the next stage of the story that we see that the church in Antioch was planted and established without any direct support from the apostles, just as the Ethiopian had been converted without their preaching. Once again, after the apostles have done their authenticating work the gospel makes its own, unimpeded progress. If that sounds automatic, even magical, remember the summary verse to which this section heads: that 'the word of God continued to increase and spread' (Acts 12:24). As some say, the word of God is the hero of Acts.

Nevertheless, the Christians in Antioch are anything but passive. Although the church has scattered, the apostles still use Jerusalem as home base. Notice here the travelling between the two places:

- Evangelists, fleeing Jerusalem, arrive in Antioch (11:19–21).
- News travels from Antioch to Jerusalem (11:22a).
- Barnabas travels from Jerusalem to Antioch (11:22b).
- Barnabas is based at Antioch, recruits Saul from Tarsus, and they stay a year working together in Antioch (11:23–25).

So far, apart from the news travelling back, the impetus has all been one way, with Jerusalem in the driving seat. But now there is a sudden dramatic turn:

- Prophets travel from Jerusalem to Antioch, warning of a famine back in Judea (11:27–28).
- Saul and Barnabas are sent as messengers *from Antioch to Jerusalem*, with financial aid (11:29–30).

For the first time in the story, the tide flows back; Jerusalem ceases to be the supportive parent and becomes an equal partner. Jerusalem still has one more dramatic role to play in releasing the churches, but a pattern has been established. The next two stories explore that new relationship.

Jerusalem: 12:1–19a

James has been arrested, imprisoned, tried and executed. The Christians in Jerusalem, and Luke's first-time readers, would assume the same pattern will apply to Peter too. Once Peter has been arrested and imprisoned his future seems clear, if only for Herod to win favour with the mob. He was neither a Jew nor a real king, but a Roman puppet and deeply unpopular.

Yet, despite the odds, the apostle is miraculously released and restored to the Christian family, before leaving Jerusalem fast. What does this say about the developing story?

- That opposition to the church is hardening and is now a useful tool for Herod to use in increasing his own standing. From this point on, it will not be the religious leaders only but the Roman judiciary that the Christians face.
- The definition of the church is sharpening. Because of developments elsewhere, particularly in Antioch, it accepts uncircumcised Gentiles as full members, and that means it can no longer have protection as a sect within Judaism.
- Jerusalem is an increasingly dangerous place to be a Christian.
- God will not let his church die, although the individual members of it may suffer horribly.
- Prayer is answered: it is characteristic of the church in Acts that it is frequently (although not always) found praying before a mighty act of God.

Caesarea: 12:19b–23

Herod and the people form an unholy alliance to oppose the gospel, and the reader is left wondering what God's reaction to that will be. The people are in no doubt about which master they serve, because when Herod addresses them as their king (12:21) they deify him, saying 'This is the voice of a god, not a man' (12:23). We should notice, by the way, the deliberate contrast between two groups as they face the famine: the church will survive because of the love between the churches, where Herod and the national leaders attempt to survive by political manoeuvring. So here are two rival kings – two rival gods, even – in Herod and Jesus, one unable to support his people, the other caring for them with generosity. There is rivalry but no competition, as the angel shows God's verdict and Herod dies, eaten by worms.

The common thread

Pulling this into shape, then, we have two main stories with principal characters – 9:32 – 11:18 being Peter and Cornelius, 12:1–23 being Peter and Herod – and an interlude in Antioch, 11:19–30. Each of the main stories has a principal theme: the first is the blessing of God on believing Gentiles (Cornelius and his family), and the second is the judgment of God on unbelieving Israel (Herod and his nation). Both receive a double, supernatural authentication: Peter and Cornelius both have a vision; Peter and Herod are both visited by an angel. And both conclude with an acknowledgment by Peter: 'I now realize how true it is that God does not show favouritism but accepts men from every nation who fear him and do what is right' (10:34–35); and 'Now I know without a doubt that the Lord sent his angel and rescued me from Herod's clutches and from everything the Jewish people were anticipating' (12:11).

In case that seems too cut and dried, with believing Gentiles and unbelieving Jews, we should remember that Peter, the apostles and the church in Jerusalem were believing Jews, and that the Roman state, which will be an increasingly major player in Acts, comprises unbelieving Gentiles. Furthermore, the relationship between the church in Antioch and the church in Jerusalem shows us both believing Jews accepting believing Gentiles and believing Gentiles actively supporting believing Jews. The gospel and racism are polar opposites.

But there is a question which Luke has left hanging in the air. What has happened to Saul, Barnabas and the money? That is how the next section starts, as the Gentile mission, freed from having to see Jerusalem as the mother church, can move ahead unimpeded.

7 | The normal pattern established:
12:25 – 16:5

Introduction

A second half
With this section Acts moves into its second half, marked by an increase in four areas:

- *Gentile converts*, once the dust has settled from the normalization of the Antioch experiment.
- *Jewish opposition*, which becomes much more programmatic and even attempts to pre-empt Paul's ministry.
- *Geographical spread*, from Jerusalem in 12:25 to Rome in 28:14.
- *Theological clarity*, especially in the Council of Jerusalem in chapter 15.

A new section
This new section mostly clusters around the ministries of Paul and Barnabas, although in 15:39 they go their separate ways. There are two principal topics:

- *Paul and Barnabas' first missionary journey: 13:1 – 14:28.* It is worth consulting a map to see where they are travelling, but the significance is again theological. It is a journey from Antioch and back to Antioch, taking in Cyprus and Asia Minor. Antioch is demonstrating its new role as the centre for the Gentile mission.
- *The Council of Jerusalem: 15:1–35.* Once again, Luke takes his readers on a journey that begins and ends in Antioch.

It would seem neat for Luke to close his section there, but he actually begins the next missionary journey in 15:36 – 16:4, travelling from Antioch to Derbe. It is possible that this is again a geographical decision, because as far as Derbe Paul is revisiting churches which were covered in the first journey. In that case, Paul would have been seen visiting the same places three times: first to evangelize and plant a church; secondly to strengthen that church; and thirdly to give that church the letter from the Council of Jerusalem. In that sense the delivery of the letter should be seen as the end of the first missionary journey, rather than the beginning of the second.

Lying behind the geography, as always, is the theological matter. The Council of Jerusalem occurred (15:1–3) because Paul and Barnabas had disagreed with others over the appropriateness of circumcision for male Gentile believers. Paul and Barnabas argued that it was a matter of freedom, and the Council agreed. It is then surprising, if not seriously shocking, to discover that in 16:1–3 Paul arranged for Timothy to be circumcised. It is in part to show that freedom on this matter really does mean freedom either way that Luke includes it in this section, as part of the consequence of the Council.

So, even though Luke recounts the apparent start of the second missionary journey, it is fair to say that the structure is:

- 13:1 – 14:28: the first missionary journey
- 15:1 – 16:4: the Council of Jerusalem and the delivery of the letter to those converted on that first journey
- 16:5: conclusion.

And the balance between the two main parts is the travelling to and from Antioch.

The first missionary journey: 13:1 – 14:28

The route for this journey is quite straightforward: across Cyprus, up the main road through Perga to Lystra and back. Luke has structured his material so that the encounters on the way raise exactly the issue that the Council will have to resolve.

Cyprus: 13:4–12

Paul began, as was his usual habit, by moving first to the synagogue, to meet the Jews there and to teach (13:5). At the other end of the island he met a Jewish false prophet and a Jewish sorcerer, Elymas – sorcery being, by contrast with going to the synagogue, a very *un*-orthodox practice. The proconsul, Sergius Paulus, wanted to hear Paul, but the sorcerer opposed it, at which he was immediately miraculously blinded. Sergius Paulus, by contrast, believes Paul rather than the false prophet, and he believes not because of the miracle but (v. 12) because of the teaching. Various themes emerge as Paul encounters this interested Gentile:

• Judaism at its worst tries to stop the gospel spreading to the Gentiles;
• Elymas moves from physical sight to physical blindness;
• Sergius Paulus moves from spiritual blindness to spiritual sight.

Therefore Judaism *at its worst* cannot prevent the gospel spreading. This is the first described encounter between Paul and a Gentile unbeliever in Acts, and it proves to be formative.

Perga: 13:13

Two features are worth noticing about this strange scene. The first is that no preaching of any kind is mentioned, which is unusual in Acts. Secondly, John Mark heads back to Jerusalem (not, as we might expect, to Antioch). It is a controversial scene. Was John Mark weak and home-loving? Was he not able to keep up the pace, or was Paul overbearing in his demands? Or perhaps the issue had to do with what had just occurred on Cyprus. We must remember that these were still early days for the conversion of the Gentiles, and maybe the implications of what John Mark saw in the freedom offered to the Gentiles troubled him. Perhaps their disagreement was theological rather than personal, and gives a foretaste of issues to come. All this is speculation, however plausible, but the result was that the team now comprised only Paul and Barnabas.

Inland to Pisidian Antioch: 13:14–52

This is not, Luke helpfully reminds us, the Antioch where the journey began, but a different one altogether. Here Paul went to a synagogue, and Luke records the sermon. Observe that, although Paul has visited synagogues before and will do so again, this is the only occasion when Luke tells us what he said. In a consistent pattern, whereby he tells us only once what was said in a context that recurred many times, we are left to conclude that this was Paul's normal evangelistic sermon in a synagogue.

- *Leadership (16–23).* Paul begins with the question of the leadership of Israel: God led them; the judges led them; Saul led them; and David led them. Now, in one of David's descendants (v. 23), God has provided a new king, the Saviour Jesus.
- *Herald (24–25).* John the Baptist's role was to announce the forthcoming king.
- *The cross and resurrection (26–31).* Then follows what Luke has been presenting as the standard apostolic gospel outline: they killed him (26–29); God raised him (30); and witnesses saw him (31).
- *The cross and resurrection foretold (32–41).* Paul concludes in precisely the way Peter had on the day of Pentecost, proving the necessity of both the cross and resurrection from the Old Testament, and even (in verse 35) using the same psalm as Peter to make the same point: David is still dead and therefore wrote about the resurrection of someone else (Ps. 16:10; see Acts 2:27). Then follow the standard apostolic requests – repentance and faith – and the standard reason, which is the role of the risen Jesus in the forthcoming judgment (40–41).

Luke has thus clearly shown that Peter and Paul preached the same gospel, even down to their cross-references. The response is heartening, for Jews, God-fearers and Gentiles come to faith. But it is also sobering, for not everyone comes to faith, and the message provokes opposition from some Jewish authorities.

Pisidian Antioch and Paphos

Pisidian Antioch and Paphos are set up as deliberate contrasts.

- Paphos shows the worst of Judaism opposing the gospel going to the Gentiles, and being completely powerless.
- Pisidian Antioch shows the best of Judaism, biblically concerned, coming to faith in Christ.
- Pisidian Antioch shows the best of Judaism, converted, acting as a springboard for Gentile faith.
- Pisidian Antioch shows the opposition of Judaism also acting as a springboard for Gentile faith.

So 13:46 is a key to understanding Paul's strategy in 13:47: the gospel goes to Jews first, and either their conversion or their refusal acts as a means for the gospel to go to the Gentiles. It is exactly in line with how Paul argues at length in Romans 9 – 11.

One unintended part of the pattern is that Paul and Barnabas were kicked out of the building by those who refused to accept the message. They would discover that this, too, was a common occurrence for them.

Iconium: 14:1–7

Here the pattern follows what happened in Pisidian Antioch: Paul preached in the synagogue, some accepted the message; Gentiles then heard the message; again some accepted it; but those who rejected the message in the synagogue ensured that Paul and Barnabas left. Luke is using his standard technique of repetition to show what was normal and reproducible. This was Paul's way of working.

Lystra: 14:8–20a

At Lystra, by contrast, the pattern is interrupted. Paul preaches as usual, and a man is converted and physically healed. But the response of the crowd to Paul is very far from the norm. They deify, idolize and attempt to sacrifice to Paul and Barnabas (vv. 11–14). This is quite different to the previous pattern of either faith or rejection; so Paul's message is not the usual gospel presentation that we might have come to expect. Instead he preaches an impromptu sermon on idolatry and the living God, and the crowd responds by turning from adulation to ugly mob violence, forcing Paul and Barnabas to leave. That complete turnaround is produced, in part, by some of the opposition to Paul from Antioch (probably Pisidian Antioch) stirring up the rabble. Organized religion forms an ugly alliance with idolatry to try to suppress the gospel.

Is this Paul's normal evangelistic method with Gentiles? Obviously not, although he naturally uses the opportunity. He speaks to the crowd on their terms and with their worldviews and explains the gospel in a fresh way. That much, at least, is normal: a normal flexibility to the audience. And people were converted – notice that in verse 20 there were 'disciples', and in verse 22 he returns to strengthen 'the disciples'. So the gospel still changes lives, even when Paul is forced to think on his feet in a hostile climate.

We need to pause again and see the cumulative case that Luke is making:

- Paphos – Judaism at its worst
- Pisidian Antioch – Judaism at its best
- Iconium – Judaism and the Gentiles at their most typical
- Lystra – Gentile culture at its most ignorant, idolatrous and murderous.

Usually, there are converts from both groupings (Lystra being the exception, perhaps because there was no synagogue mentioned for Paul to go to first) and opposition from both groupings.

Derbe: 14:20a–21a

Derbe is, for the moment, the end of the road, but it is here in part to show that none of the opposition in Lystra will divert Paul and Barnabas' mission. Despite hostility, the gospel still advances.

The road home: 14:21b–28

This section shows Paul and Barnabas deliberately retracing their steps, revisiting each of the churches. This time (with one exception) the focus is not on reaching non-Christians but on 'strengthening the disciples and encouraging them to remain true to the faith' (14:22). The mounting pressure was obviously causing some concern, and so each church is given the message about the inevitability of hardship for Christian believers, and then elders, to teach and lead the congregation, are appointed. Luke would want us to notice, then, that the hardship Paul and Barnabas were experiencing was not atypical, but a normal pattern for believers, and perhaps especially for the leaders they were appointing in each place (see 20:18–35, the relevant comments, and the sermon 'Wolves in Shepherds' Clothing', chapter 16 p. 157).

The exception to the pattern of focusing on maturing believers occurs at Perga in Pamphylia. That had been the place where John Mark had left the mission team after the trip to Cyprus (13:13), and perhaps they had been so absorbed in that issue that evangelism had not taken place. This time, however, they 'preached the word' there, and returned back to Antioch to tell their sending church of the remarkable work God had been doing.

What marks this section out has been the growing normality of approaching Jews and Gentiles on an equal footing, with explicitly the same gospel. This will inevitably explode in the questions: how Jewish does a Gentile Christian have to be, and how free from Jewish tradition may a Jewish Christian be? The second half of this section, in the Council of Jerusalem, showed how this question was answered for the most fundamental of Jewish distinctives: circumcision, the mark of belonging to the covenant family.

The Council of Jerusalem: 15:1 – 16:4

The circumcision question explodes, appropriately enough, in Antioch, the home of the Jew–Gentile Christian phenomenon. The exact status of these men has been long debated, and it is still not clear. Perhaps Luke intended to be slightly opaque in order to spare the blushes of some people who changed their minds during the Council. Clearly, though, the church was being targeted by some senior outsiders, and of all the theories surrounding the date of Galatians, those which picture it occurring in the heat of this particular crisis, at this moment, have most to commend them. In this case, the leadership behind the 'men . . . from Judea' turns out to be very senior indeed, for Paul notes that it was only after 'certain men came from James' that even Peter gave in to their pressure (Gal. 2:12). Paul and Barnabas were involved in 'sharp dispute and debate' with them, and the result was a high-level crisis that needed a prominent and effective solution. Paul and Barnabas were sent from Antioch to contribute.

The Council

The issue is clearly there in verse 5: 'The Gentiles must be circumcised and required to obey the law of Moses'. But the question that lies behind it is whether circumcision is a matter of custom or salvation, and that becomes clear in Peter's speech, which is his final appearance in Acts.

- *Peter speaks (15:7–11).* Whatever Peter had once temporarily yielded to, he and Paul are now absolutely at one that Gentiles are 'saved' by 'grace' (v. 11). For Peter, then, this issue is a gospel issue: how is it that Gentiles can be saved? On what terms do they enter the covenant people? His answer is that they are *not* saved by circumcision: that is, by becoming proselytes of Judaism.
- *Paul and Barnabas speak (15:12).* Paul and Barnabas give an account of how God has authenticated his work among the Gentiles, and authenticated Paul as the Apostle to the Gentiles, in exactly the way he had authenticated his work in Jerusalem with the first apostles.
- *James speaks (15:13–21).* James addresses the Council, on the basis of Amos 9:11–12. Commentaries vary on some textual points here, but the main thrust is surely that God had always intended to remake the Davidic kingdom (v. 16), and that kingdom was going to include both the remnant of believing Jews (v. 17a) and Gentiles (v. 17b), so if Gentiles believe in King Jesus, they bear his name (v. 17b) – as the Antioch believers would put it, 'We are *Christians!*'

   There is then no need for the Gentiles to become physically Jewish by circumcision, for simply by being Gentiles who bear the name of Jesus, they belong. Gentile believers are full believers, and are already God's own people (v. 14).

The decision

The application, as James speaks it (vv. 20–21) and as the decision of the Council is summarized in a letter (vv. 23–29), at first sight is odd, but in fact it is wise: of course (v. 19) these Gentile people are Christians and so of course they do not need to be circumcised. But they need to remember that Jewish Christians who have been brought up with the Old Testament laws have certain scruples over food, and the Gentiles would do well to take that into account. And in case it needed reinforcing, the freedom that the gospel brings does not give freedom for sexual indulgence.

This shows in summary form how the early church seems to have understood the nature of the continuing authority of the Old Testament laws for Christians; or rather, how it handled differences on that account. This is a critical area of controversy still, both for New Testament studies and for current moral questions. But, in outline, the response of the Council here seems to have been that there were tolerated differences and also ongoing relational and theological disagreements. For instance, Paul addresses the lack of liberty that some Christians permit others over food or Sabbath days in various churches (e.g. Rom. 14; Col. 2:16–19). The question of 'food sacrificed to idols' was a running issue in Corinth (1 Cor. 8), because there was evidently disagreement over whether particular food had been so sacrificed or not. Paul's answer there seems in line with the Council: that if someone *thinks* it has been sacrificed to an idol, it has. The weaker brother wins.

It was obviously a different matter with 'sexual immorality', although it is not possible to see that from within this letter. Paul can be relaxed about the food issue in 1 Corinthians 8, although he is clear on the underlying, relational issue, but he is far from relaxed about the sexual immorality he addresses in chapter 5. That is not an area for liberty of discussion and freedom of conscience.

This seems all to be an outworking of the teaching of Jesus in Mark 7, where Jesus denied that food has the power to make anyone spiritually 'unclean' (7:15), and declared all foods 'clean' (7:19), but with his next breath warns about a range of behaviours, including 'sexual immorality', which *do* make people 'unclean' (vv. 20–23).

So we should notice how particular are the foods that the Jerusalem Council forbids. There is nothing forbidding the eating of pork or items covered by the other food laws, only the items that seem essentially involved with the activities of idolatry, or which were involved in the preparation of any kind of meat. So a Gentile

Christian can invite a Jewish Christian to his or her home, and the Jewish Christian can eat what has been set on the table with no lingering qualms about what has happened in the kitchen. The fundamental problem of relationships has been resolved.

The letter

The letter summarizing the decision was therefore drafted and sent to Antioch, as the home of the Gentile mission (vv. 30–35), and any new converts and churches would use it as their practice. But the question remained: what then of the converts and churches *prior to* the Council? So the decision was made to revisit once more (15:36–41), and so the churches are included in this panel of Acts one more time.

The question over the inclusion of John Mark, and the parting of the ways of Paul and Barnabas, was obviously a serious one. It is worth noting that once again John Mark causes problems when the issue of Jewish and Gentile relations is in the frame, and the letter is about to be delivered; perhaps Paul was not convinced that the man had thoroughly understood, or proved his sympathy with, the strategy. But it should not be overdrawn as a conflict: Paul was not jealous of Barnabas' later influence in Corinth (1 Cor. 9:6), and Paul was confident of the later ministry of John Mark (Phlm. 24; 2 Tim. 4:11). There was no theological issue here, and they were responsible enough to part without dismissing each other as believers or workers. So, although the split was undeniably sad, and we cannot pass any verdict on the wisdom of either man, the result was two missionary teams rather than one. This perhaps gave the church the idea for the next stage of multiplying ministries.

The implications

The final scene in this panel is encouraging, on first sight, for it shows that the early church was not short of talented younger leaders, and Paul was able to add Timothy to his new team and to start the next stage of the mission with a training element added.

But there is another element which is curious: having fought the tough fight in Antioch and Jerusalem for the freedom of Gentiles not to be circumcised, and to make it crystal clear that everyone is saved by grace alone, it seems eccentric of Paul to have Timothy, a Gentile, circumcised. Luke makes this scene so prominent after the Council that we must still be seeing the outworking of its principles, of which there seem to be two.

First, there is the principle of freedom. That Gentiles have the freedom not to be circumcised can easily turn into a custom, or even a law. 'I am a Gentile Christian', someone says, 'and so I have not been circumcised.' That, of course, is not freedom at all but a new law. Therefore, to show that the Council intended that the decision was a genuinely free one, Timothy is circumcised quite voluntarily.

Secondly, there is the principle of flexibility. Luke notes that Timothy's father was Greek and his mother was Jewish. As a Gentile, whether he was circumcised or not was irrelevant, but even though he was Jewish on his mother's side, his uncircumcised state meant he would not be accepted as a teacher in a synagogue and therefore could not take the evangelistic opportunities Paul used and had chosen him for. In order to win a hearing with non-Christians, he freely submitted to circumcision. It is an outworking of the spirit underlying the letter from the Council.

This panel of Acts has raised a critical question: on what terms may a Gentile be saved? And the clear answer is, on equal terms with a Jew: namely, through grace, and with gospel-controlled freedom with regard to the law.

8 | The unchanging gospel in a world of cultures: 16:6 – 19:20

Introduction

Once again, as we look at a long section, we should start with the idea that Luke planned his material carefully. We have seen that he wrote down neither a stream of ideas as they came to his head, nor everything that happened in the early church. Rather, it is legitimate to ask questions about plan and purpose. Four elements hold this section together and give it a sense of development.

1. Geography

This time, the panel takes us beyond the confines of the churches visited in the first missionary journey. A new field of work opens up, as God guides the missionaries into continental Europe. This new area comprises three Roman provinces, which shape the sequence of events: Macedonia (16:6 – 17:15), Achaia (17:16 – 18:17) and Asia (18:18 – 19:19), with a concluding verse at 19:20. Luke's control is seen in the narrowing focus: in Macedonia he reports from three places (Philippi, Thessalonica and Berea); in Achaia from two (Athens and Corinth); and in Asia, only from Ephesus. Ephesus, then, should be seen as the climax of this phase of ministry.

2. Theology

As we have consistently seen in Acts, geography is never a matter of map references, but of understanding the world under the reign of the risen Jesus. So, in this panel, God is explicitly at work in moving the missionaries on and confirming that in each province they are there according to his plan. After having been prevented from preaching in Asia 'by the Holy Spirit' (16:6) and forbidden to go to Bithynia 'by the Spirit of Jesus' (16:7), they are forced to wait on the coast at Troas until they can move to Macedonia as a result of a vision (16:8–10), 'concluding that God had called us to preach the gospel to them' (16:10). Despite opposition, Paul and the team remain in Corinth as the result of a second vision (18:9–11). And he refuses to engage in extensive work in Ephesus until he is persuaded that it is 'God's will' (18:21). In the light of God's earlier forbidding Paul to travel to Ephesus, he must mean more than a casual 'if God permits it'. He needs as explicit a permission to go as he had an earlier ban.

3. Ministry

Luke has already shown Paul's flexibility with gospel messages, and that continues in this section. The message to the synagogue in Thessalonica (17:1–4) has a markedly different feel to the one in Athens shortly afterwards (17:22–31), although readers need to take care to remember Luke's techniques of compression and repetition as those sermons are compared.

What is new in this section is Luke's careful monitoring of the time that Paul spends in each place. The time-scale definitely changes, as can be seen from the list in Table 8.1. It seems reasonable to conclude that Paul spent increasing amounts of time in each place, where he had the freedom to choose, and that intensive time was increasingly spent with Gentiles. Whether that is because there was less opposition, so it was possible, or he encountered greater ignorance, so it was necessary, or a combination, is impossible to say. It is also worth considering that the closer he travelled to Rome, the harder it would be to disguise the fact that, even though the new faith in Jesus could not claim Judaism's protected status, in a time of sudden anti-Semitic persecution (18:2), he was a Jew.

Philippi	16:12	Several days.
Thessalonica	17:2	A maximum of four weeks, minimum of a fortnight.
Berea	17:11–13	No time mentioned, but there is no stress on urgency, and there is a note of extended and intensive evangelism.
Athens	17:16	Paul is waiting, and no time-scale is given.
Corinth	18:11	Eighteen months.
Ephesus	19:8	Three months with the Jews.
	19:10	Two years with the Greeks.

Table 8.1

4. Opposition

Opposition was not new, of course, and there were continued attempts at impromptu opposition in Thessalonica (17:5) and Berea (17:13). But it takes a new form in this section as it tries to organize itself legally: for the first time, Paul found himself in court. His encounter with Sergius Paulus on Cyprus was a private matter, even though the latter was a proconsul (13:7). In Philippi, though, Paul came before the magistrates because of a Gentile accusation (16:20), and in Corinth he came before the proconsul, Gallio, because of a Jewish accusation (18:12–13). There are other cases, too, such as in Thessalonica, where Jason and others were arrested. But in both Philippi and Corinth Paul was in court, and released. The Roman system did not find him guilty under either Roman (16:37–40) or Jewish law (18:15). This theme will become particularly critical in the final panel of Acts, which contains Paul's three legal defences.

So much for the themes. We turn now to the narrative.

The Macedonian ministry: 16:6 – 17:15

Acts 16:10 marks an intriguing moment, when Luke ceases to talk simply of 'Paul and his companions' (16:6) and reveals that he was there for this part of the story: 'we got ready to leave'. He does not make anything of the information, other than to reinforce for

Theophilus and his other readers that for this part at least he did not need to do research, because it was his turn to be an 'eye-witness' (Luke 1:2).

Philippi: 16:6–40

The stories are familiar. Paul went outside Philippi to find his first Jewish hearers. It needed ten Jewish men to form a synagogue; if there were not enough for that, then the custom was to meet near flowing waters on the Sabbath. Synagogues seem to have begun during the exile, where, as the Psalmist said,

> By the rivers of Babylon we sat and wept
>> when we remembered Zion.
>
> (Ps. 137:1)

Away from the homeland, then, Lydia and a few other Jews met to encourage one another, and that is where Paul explained the gospel, and 'the Lord opened her heart to respond to Paul's message' (16:14). Some time after that a slave girl was exorcized, and although no mention is made of her conversion it seems a reasonable inference, and finally Paul and Silas are imprisoned, and the jailer is converted.

This, then, is how Paul evangelizes after the Council of Jerusalem. He had written in Galatians that 'there is neither Jew nor Greek, slave nor free, male nor female' when it comes to justification by faith (Gal. 3:24–29), and here is the outworking: Jew, Greek, slave, free, male and female were all reached in Philippi. If it is the case that the middle story was a conversion as well as an exorcism, then that is an example of three categories in one: a Gentile slave woman. So when Paul gathers the church in Philippi (16:40) we are to see it as a model church, living out the pattern of the Council and its letter.

Thessalonica and Berea: 17:1–15

Having seen Paul's method where there was no synagogue, here is his method when there was, in a contrasting pair of cities.

Luke tells us that Paul acted 'as his custom was' (17:2) and in five words 'reasoned . . . explaining . . . proving . . . proclaiming' and 'persuad[ing]' about Jesus, the suffering and risen Christ, from one source, 'the Scriptures'. That happened at three Sabbath meetings in the synagogue, and no doubt on countless informal occasions as well. We must conclude that Paul did this in Berea, too, since it was his 'custom', and that Luke is making a deliberate contrast. On the one hand the Bereans 'received the message with great eagerness and examined the Scriptures every day to see if what Paul said was true' (17:11), and on the other the Thessalonians, or at least some of them, 'were jealous . . . formed a mob and started a riot' (17:5). There was gospel fruit in both places, though, and Luke shows us 'some' who were 'persuaded' in Thessalonica (17:4) and 'many' who 'believed' in Berea (17:12): men and women, Jews and Greeks. So when Luke takes us to the synagogue to watch Paul teaching there, we see that when people study the Scriptures honestly, rather than with an eye to their own reputation (17:5), the gospel bears fruit. Notice too, though, that the opposition to Paul followed him from Thessalonica to Berea, meaning that even when there is a favourable response there will be hostility. Luke is preparing us for the fact that although there will be much Jewish faith, the hostility of some Jews who do not believe will determine his fate.

The Achaean ministry: 17:16 – 18:17

Athens

Yet again Paul visited the synagogue, with his standard approach (17:17), sketched in lightly by Luke because we know by now how the teaching will have been given. Much more extensively, Luke reports Paul's encounter with pagan culture: his only extended and thought-through sermon to Gentiles in Acts. If the idea is right that Luke reports once what was said typically, then this may have been a sermon that was used on many other occasions in encountering the culture.

To understand it, we need to understand the city he was speaking to and the voice he used. We need to grasp just how significant is the target Paul has chosen: Athens was – is – the city of Sophocles and Aeschylus, of Socrates and Plato, Pericles and Phidias. If those names mean little or nothing, they were among the Athenian men who pioneered the West's basic understandings of theatre, philosophy, democratic government and architecture. Those words – theatre, philosophy, democracy and architecture – are Greek words, showing their abiding contribution. In many other fields too, such as sculpture, medicine, public speaking or the writing of history, the Athenians arrived there not only first, but in such a dominating way that even today we are still in their shadow. The building in which I work has an entrance porch obviously drawn on Greek architecture. So when Paul criticized the idolatry of Athens, he was criticizing the best of the West.

It is essential to capture his tone here, the second feature of his sermon. Paul was not in awe of the marvels of ancient Greece, as tourists then were and today still are, nor filled with gentle reason, acknowledging Athens' intellectual strengths and contribution but pointing out some weaknesses. This was a head-on critique.

The line of his thinking is to move from God as the only creator and ongoing sustainer of everything and everyone, the Father who loves his lost children and the Judge who, on the last day, will rule. The motif of the Last Day is where Paul was asked to head all the time, because he had been asked to speak about 'the good news about Jesus and the resurrection' (17:18), and the message finishes on the note of the 'resurrection' (vv. 31–32). Although this conclusion is brief, it still fits in with the standard gospel proclamation: Jesus was a 'man' who was 'dead' (i.e. they killed him); by 'raising him from the dead' (God raised him) God has given 'proof' (witnesses saw him) of the coming judgment and possible salvation. So it would be reasonable to think that Luke has carefully condensed this part of the message for his readers, because we already know what the message is on those points, in order to focus on the first part of the message.

It is a deeply negative message: God, despite the fact they have built him temples, 'does not live in temples built by hands' (17:24). And, despite the regiments of religious staff who served at those temples, 'he is not served by human hands' (17:25). In fact the beautiful architecture of Athens is an idol which blinds them to the fact that, far from God needing them to build a house for him to dwell in and be served by, 'he himself gives all men life and . . . everything else' (17:24–25). The beautiful art of Athens, and the philosophy and mythology that lay behind it, is mere 'ignorance' (17:30). 'We should not think' like that (17:29). Even their cultivated and urbane way of including an altar to an 'unknown god' (17:23), which looks so seemingly modest and open, actually ignores the fact that God wants us to know him, and has both acted and spoken in 'proof' of that (17:31). Cultivated Athens, known for its wisdom, is actually ignorant after all. See the linked sermon, 'Why intelligent people can also be stupid' (p. 147).

Corinth

Corinth shows the standard approach to both Jews and Gentiles, but this time the bad feeling seems to start earlier, perhaps because it is snowballing as Paul's opponents track him down and perhaps even anticipate his moves. But God tells Paul that, despite the increasingly strong attempts to block him, the gospel will still do its work, and that because he has a specific task to do, God will protect him. So the case is thrown out.

Athens and Corinth

It is tempting to contrast the situations in Athens and Corinth in a way that misses the point, by noticing a cool, intellectual approach in the one and a passionate, non-intellectual one in the other. The evidence for an intellectual approach in Athens is drawn from this part of Acts, and the contrast is drawn from 1 Corinthians, where Paul says:

> When I came to you, brothers, I did not come with eloquence or superior wisdom as I proclaimed to you the testimony about God. For I resolved to know nothing while I was with you except Jesus Christ and him crucified. I came to you in weakness and fear, and with much trembling. My message and my preaching were not with wise and persuasive words, but with a demonstration of the Spirit's power, so that your faith might not rest on men's wisdom, but on God's power.
> (1 Cor. 2:1–5)

So, it is sometimes said, Paul changed his mind midway from Athens to Corinth: at the former he used 'eloquence . . . superior wisdom . . . wise and persuasive words', and by the time of the latter had 'resolved' to use nothing but 'Jesus Christ and him crucified . . . weakness and fear . . . trembling' and 'the Spirit's power'. Athens, it is alleged, showed Paul's last attempt at rational, programmed evangelism, which was a failure, and Corinth showed a much less rational, spiritually based form of evangelism, which showed evident success.

There is, undoubtedly, a contrast between the two cities, for in Athens 'a few men . . . believed' (although that is more than it sounds, for 'among them was Dionysus, a member of the Areopagus, also a woman named Damaris, and a number of others' [17:34]), while in Corinth (18:8) 'many of the Corinthians who heard him believed and were baptised'. There is a difference between 'few' and 'many'. Nevertheless, we should be careful here. Bringing material in from 1 Corinthians and comparing it with Acts, with two different authors involved, is highly problematic.

On the 1 Corinthians side, this comparison depends on a highly ironic part of the letter, and Paul is using a careful rhetorical strategy. 'Eloquence', 'superior wisdom' and 'wise and persuasive words' were actually ideals that the Corinthians valued, not the Athenians, and much of 1 Corinthians is designed to explode their love of such concepts. Equally, the cross is something the Corinthians have forgotten, not Paul. Athens is not in his mind at all here, and we should be wary of taking such highly loaded terms from one New Testament book and using them as if they were neutral in tone.

On the Acts side, we must remember that Luke has his own literary strategy, and he does not show Paul changing his mind at all on this matter. Exactly the opposite is the case, for when he came to Corinth, 'every Sabbath he *reasoned* in the synagogue, *trying to persuade* Jews and Greeks. When Silas and Timothy came from Macedonia, Paul devoted himself exclusively to *preaching, testifying* to the Jews that Jesus was the Christ.' Luke seems deliberately to be showing that Paul had not changed his evangelistic method at all.

So, if there is a contrast between Athens and Corinth, and it does not lie outside Acts but within what Luke intended to write, where is it? It seems to lie in two misunderstandings:

- *The misunderstanding in Athens* (17:18) was that Paul was thought to be advocating foreign gods, Jesus and the resurrection – perhaps thought to be a goddess, his consort, called Anastasia? There was, of course, nothing illegal or treacherous in that, but Paul was concerned that his hearers understand that the gospel is a claim to absolute truth and cannot tolerate being an equal partner in a multi-faith experiment.

- *The misunderstanding in Corinth* (18:13) was that Paul was alleged to be advocating an illegal god. Whether the charge was that he was causing disturbances between Jews, or that he was falsely hiding behind a mask of Judaism, is not clear and does not matter at this point. It is enough that, just as he was misunderstood in Athens, he was also misunderstood in Corinth. If Paul's opponents wished to have Paul arrested and brought to trial, the lesson for them was that the case would have to be very carefully constructed, for Rome was notoriously relaxed about any multitude of religions unless they claimed ultimate status.

The Asian ministry: 18:18 – 19:19

Luke tells the story of the Ephesian ministry with great care. In 18:18–21 Paul visited Ephesus briefly and then returned to Antioch. That marks the end of the second missionary journey, which started as the delivery of the Jerusalem letter and then included the circumcision of Timothy, ending the previous panel (16:1–4). This shows that Luke is not writing a simple history of the missionary journeys, but something more programmatic.

Paul, then, returned to Antioch and then revisited the Galatian churches again: his fourth such visit (18:23). But Luke's principal interest at this point lies in Ephesus, and that is where he draws our attention with three stories: one where Paul is absent (but Apollos is present) and two when he is present. It would be neat to contrast them with the three Philippian stories that opened this panel, and certainly there is again a stress on converted Jews and exorcism. But what they have in common is probably more obviously a theme: they all involve some degree of distortion of the gospel, moving from quite mild to extremely dangerous.

Apollos: 18:24–28
Luke underlines Apollos' knowledge of Scripture and the gospel of Jesus, which he taught 'accurately' (18:25), but clearly there is something defective in that he 'knew only the baptism of John'. This is

clearly a milder problem than the next one we encounter, for Apollos is not rebaptized, nor does he need to receive the Holy Spirit; he merely needs to be 'taught . . . more adequately' (18:26). Whatever the gaps in his knowledge that were filled, the results of his ministry subsequently lay in Achaia. That was of course where Paul had just been, and Paul reflected on that double ministry of the two men in Corinth when he wrote 'I planted the seed, Apollos watered it, but God made it grow' (1 Cor. 3:6).

The twelve disciples: 19:1–7

When Paul encountered these men he asked an odd question: 'Did you receive the Holy Spirit when you believed?' (19:2). It is an odd question, because believing the gospel and yet not receiving the Spirit is a highly unusual, and theologically significant event. It was what had happened to the Samaritans in chapter 8. Like Apollos, they know 'the baptism of John' (18:25; 19:3), but since John's ministry and baptism announced that Jesus would baptize people in the Holy Spirit (Luke 3:16), it seems the depth of their ignorance left them unconverted.

The solution may lie in the distance between Ephesus and Palestine. Perhaps these people had been baptized by John and then had to leave the land before the ministry of Jesus had begun, so that the news of Jesus' death and resurrection (assuming that they had even heard of it) would mean nothing to them. All they knew was to wait.

It is probably best to see these people as living in a historical time-warp: even though Jesus had come, they were still waiting for him, because they left Israel at the wrong time. They answer a question which must have been common at this stage of the church's history: how do you reach someone who responded obediently to John, but never heard about Jesus? Paul modelled the way.

The result is that Paul had the nucleus of a church in Ephesus, and when he had to leave the synagogue and set up in a lecture room, he already had a favourable crowd to bring friends and contacts along. With all the travel surrounding Ephesus and the towns in its influence, it is surely no exaggeration for Luke to report that after two years 'all the Jews and Greeks who lived in the province of Asia heard the word of the Lord' (19:10).

The seven sons of Sceva: 19:11–19

This story, the third distortion, is quite different in feel and tone from the previous two. It shares with them an innocent intention but is quite different, because these men, who were not Christians and had no intention of becoming Christians, were trying to appropriate the benefits of the Holy Spirit. They were not greedy or ambitious like Simon Magus (8:9–24), and they were clearly trying to do good, impressed by the fact that the Jesus Paul proclaimed was obviously not a mere philosophical concept but a God who is alive and powerful (19:11–12).

Ephesus was an occult centre, so it would be possible to call this some kind of 'power encounter', but we should notice in that case what was happening. This was neither planned nor witnessed by Paul, who is nowhere in the story. Nor is the principal supernatural actor, the Holy Spirit. Rather, the Evil One responds to the name of Jesus, even though no believer is present. Both this and the miraculous handkerchiefs in the previous verses, which set the scene, are examples of the power of God at work a distance from the ministry of Paul, although in the main story God's power lies in the superstitious attempt of the men to control it and the laughter of the demon as it realizes that these men do not have the authority they claim and which it fears.

We learn, then, that there is a place for 'spiritual warfare', but that it is God who engages with it, and our role is not to become fascinated by it, for that is the pagan's mindset, nor to work strategically for it. Paul's reticence here is quite remarkable. Neither the miracle of the handkerchiefs nor the opposition of Satan is something Paul courted, and apparently it was enough for him to preach the message. That is powerful enough, for the gospel and Satan are opposites and repel. In some places the opposition is intellectual and cultural, as in Athens, and sometimes it is more explicitly at work, as here. Whether the results are few conversions or many; whether we are met by rational scepticism, religious jealousy, political manoeuvring or credulous superstition; or whether the message produces genuine miracles, supernatural opposition or deep personal conversion, the message, throughout this panel, has remained the same, for it is 'the word of the Lord' (19:20).

9 | To Rome: 19:21 – 28:31

This panel is odd. What more does Luke have to say? Why does he not finish his story with the apparent success in Ephesus, rather than the downbeat note in Rome? There are a number of themes that have preoccupied Luke about which we hear nothing more. Paul's teaching to non-Christians, while it continues in this section, is not expanded in any new way. Nor is Paul's strategy in church planting or training. There is one major speech to church leaders gathered at Miletus in 20:18–35, but on the quite reasonable suggestion that this was, in its bare bones, the message that Paul frequently gave to leaders, Luke could easily have tucked it in elsewhere. So why does he write this long panel of Acts, which takes up nearly one-third of the book, and which includes a quite elaborate description of a storm and a shipwreck?

One possibility is that the new element in this panel is to see Paul defend the gospel against charges. Luke has earlier shown that Paul was about to face this danger, in Philippi and Corinth (16:19–24; 18:12–16), but this is the time he reports what occurred. Paul passed through a sequence of investigations, informal hearings and trials, and Luke shows how he was innocent of the three key charges made against him. As he said before Festus (25:8), 'I have done nothing wrong against the law of the Jews or against the temple or against Caesar.'

- *The law of the Jews.* This would particularly have concerned his teaching, and especially with regard to the centrality of Jesus' resurrection, both for who he is and our accountability to him. It would also have raised the questions of whether Gentiles need to adhere to circumcision and the food laws.
- *The temple.* This would have flowed on from those last elements, in Paul's apparently bringing an uncircumcised Gentile into the Jerusalem temple (21:27–29).
- *Caesar.* Riots and political disturbances had dogged Paul's footsteps and would continue to do so.

It is too strong to say that Acts was constructed as Paul's defence for his trial in Rome, but if (more generally) part of the purpose of Acts is to defend the gospel before sceptical non-believers who have heard that Christianity is a troublemaking and illegal faith, then this might in part explain the length of this section and its concern with legal niceties.

To keep attention on the major flow of this section, it is helpful to look at *nine aspects* of it.

1. The story

Geography is once again a helpful ally, as it shows that there are five phases to this sequence. Because the panel is so long, it may be helpful to summarize the key events in each section.

From Ephesus to Jerusalem: 19:21 – 21:16
The key verse is 19:21:

> After all this had happened, Paul decided to go to Jerusalem, passing through Macedonia and Achaia. 'After I have been there,' he said, 'I must visit Rome also.'

This gives the programme for all of this section, and indeed to the end of Acts.

The events in this section are briefly summarized: there was a riot in Ephesus, because of the success of Paul in speaking against the idolatry and superstition of the city (19:23–41), after which followed a truncated ministry in Macedonia and Greece (20:1–3), shortened by both the opposition against him and his desire to travel to Jerusalem and Rome. Passing back through, he met the elders of the Ephesian church at Miletus (20:13–38); the meeting was there rather than at the provincial capital because 'he was in a hurry to reach Jerusalem, if possible, by the day of Pentecost' (20:16). He travelled to Jerusalem along the coast, and 'in every city the Holy Spirit' warned Paul 'that prison and hardships are facing' him (20:23). That was certainly repeated in Tyre (21:4) and Caesarea (21:10–12).

This journey, then is at God's instigation, and will involve Paul in considerable hardship.

In Jerusalem: 21:17 – 23:11

For the sake of the conscience of the Jewish Christians, Paul visited the temple and fulfilled an act of (voluntary) pity, the paying of a Nazirite vow. It is worth seeing that, as with the circumcision of Timothy, Paul saw such matters as genuine freedoms, and he was completely unbound in his approach. Some Jews from Asia recognized Paul there and claimed he was bringing Gentiles into the temple, thus proving why Timothy's circumcision was such a wise move. The near-riot which followed was quelled by the quick action of a Roman commander, who allowed Paul to address the crowd at length in Aramaic. His desire to have Paul flogged was thwarted by Paul's Roman citizenship (flogging a Roman was a capital offence). Paul then addressed the Sanhedrin so that the commander could understand the point at issue, but the meeting again descended into chaos and Paul was taken into protective custody.

The forward movement continues, as God told Paul in prison in Jerusalem that 'As you have testified about me in Jerusalem, so you must also testify in Rome' (23:11). All the accidents and delays that happened to Paul along the way, then, must be taken under the general rule that God would arrange for Paul to arrive in Rome and his clear control could not be overridden.

From Jerusalem to a hearing and a lengthy wait: 23:12 – 24:27

An attempt to assassinate Paul prompted a shrewd commander to pass the buck and to send Paul, with a self-congratulatory letter, to the provincial governor in Caesarea, to get rid of him. Felix listened to the case but declined to pass judgment for two years, perhaps intending to leave the resolution of this tricky decision to his successor, and in the meanwhile to keep the support of the Jewish authorities by refusing to release Paul.

At Caesarea: 25:1 – 26:32

Felix's successor, Porcius Festus, wanted to ingratiate himself with his new people and so planned a show trial in Jerusalem. Paul's only way out of that was to prove his innocence in a risky appeal to Caesar. Festus would have had no option but to grant the request; together with King Agrippa, he heard Paul make the formal defence submission which would travel to Rome with him.

Caesarea to Rome: 27:1 – 28:28

This section describes a long journey, with a long shipwreck; on the way, Paul performed two miracles in Malta. The Christians in Rome met Paul as he approached the city (28:15), and then he was placed under house arrest. The terms of that were obviously loose enough for him to be able to preach first to Jews (not at the synagogue, for he cannot travel to them, but in his own accommodation) and then to Gentiles (28:23–28). Verses 30 and 31 thus function as the concluding verses not only of this panel, but of the entire book, showing how the kingdom of God may legitimately be preached to Jews and Gentiles under the authority of the Lord Jesus Christ.

2. Mounting opposition

The story thus far had led us to expect opposition from both Jews and Gentiles, but what this panel shows, especially in the extended speech to church leaders, is that the issue is more complex. Three new forces show themselves. First, not only will Christians and their leaders suffer, but future church leaders will themselves be the origin of much of the opposition to the gospel and the consequent troubles. Secondly, the forces of nature conspire to make Paul deviate, if not die. Thirdly, the blind course of justice in which Paul is locked make him for much of the time a passive subject in the decision-making of others.

3. God's sovereignty

Paul is repeatedly found attesting to his certainty that he *must* travel to Rome (23:11), not least in the fact that there are repeated warnings that this will result in serious hardships for him, and even death. In 21:22–23 the dynamic appears very clearly.

> And now, compelled by the Spirit, I am going to Jerusalem, not knowing what will happen to me there. I only know that in every city the Holy Spirit warns me that prison and hardships are facing me. However, I consider my life worth nothing to me, if only I may finish the race and complete the task the Lord Jesus has given me – the task of testifying to the gospel of God's grace.

He did not take the warnings from the Holy Spirit to mean that he should deny his compulsion from the same Holy Spirit that he should make the journey. So, even when those warnings came in the form of a prophecy and were followed up by the pleadings of the church, he refused to be dissuaded.

> [T]he people there pleaded with Paul not to go up to Jerusalem. Then Paul answered, 'Why are you weeping and breaking my heart? I am ready not only to be bound, but also to die in Jerusalem for the name of the Lord Jesus.' When he would not be dissuaded, we gave up and said, 'The Lord's will be done.'
> (21:12–14)

We should not miss the personal appeal in that section, because once again Luke is in the picture: '*we* . . . pleaded with Paul not to go up to Jerusalem'. Even his own travelling companions were appealing to him not to travel, yet his certainty was unshaken. Perhaps it explains the calm way he took the decision to appeal to Caesar.

4. The extended (and only) address to Christians from Paul

Paul repeatedly spoke to Christians, and Luke has repeatedly drawn attention to Paul's multiple visits to churches. Here, though, is Paul's only long address to Christian leaders, and it fits in with Luke's strategy of reporting once what was said repeatedly, for it to occur in this final panel. If the earlier speeches have shown Paul's pattern in evangelizing, this is his warranted pattern for church leadership, and it is shaped around the issue of what the Ephesian elders knew about Paul.

- *You know* the manner of my ministry (20:18–19).
- *You know* the content of my gospel (20:20–21).
- *I know* that suffering awaits me, but I am content with that (20:22–24).
- *I know* that I shall never see you again, so I reassure you that I have told you and shown you all you need to know (20:25–27).
- *I know* that there will be false teachers, so be faithful. Defend against them, and do not become one. You will be safe (20:28–32).
- *You know* that I worked hard in order to be generous, so you must do the same (20:33–35).

Luke has therefore shown us Paul's entire strategy in reaching lost people and planting and establishing churches with a view to the next generation of leaders. There is more new church work reported in Acts, and we are to follow the example. It is quite plausible that Paul was released after the end of Acts and continued further ministry, and there are certainly traditions both within and outside the New Testament which support that.[1] Those, though, lie outside Luke's determined authorial view; his story, if not Paul's, ends in Rome.

5. Defences

There are six occasions in this panel when Paul makes some kind of personal defence. Some are informal, some highly formal, and so the

---

1. See Christopher Green, *Finishing the Race: Reading 2 Timothy Today* (Sydney: Aquila Press, 2000), pp. 7–35.

status varies: they are not all equally legally flavoured. Nevertheless, there is a sense of continued pressure as he speaks:

- Before the crowd (22:1–21)
- Before the Sanhedrin (23:1–6)
- Before Felix (24:10–21)
- Before Festus (25:8–11)
- Before Festus and Agrippa (and, implicitly, before the emperor) (26:2–27)
- Before the Jews in Rome (28:25–28).

It is therefore important for Luke that Paul is innocent of the three charges of false teaching, temple abuse and rioting. His purpose in this panel is to commend the reasonableness of the gospel and its principal herald.

6. Doublets

It is quite striking how many events in this panel seem to occur on two occasions, with enough similarity to be noticeable, even though they are not repetitions. As can be seen from Table 9.1, they are substantial pairings.

Two temple riots	Ephesus and Jerusalem
Two long journeys	Ephesus to Jerusalem; and Caesarea to Rome
Two informal enquiries	Before the Sanhedrin and before Festus
Two formal trials	Before Felix and before Festus and Agrippa
Two assassination attempts	In Jerusalem and on the way to Caesarea
Two accounts of Paul's conversion	Before the crowd and before Festus and Agrippa
Two letters	One to Felix, and one which was going to be written by Agrippa (25:26)

Table 9.1

Although this is a long and complex section, once again Luke's control of material is remarkable; he is obviously determined that his readers should not become lost in the maze of detail.

7. Echoes

Those doublets should remind Luke's readers of the opening panel, which had a similar structural feature (see p. 55). Luke is thus showing that his story is completed. As we consider Table 9.2, we may even notice some similarities of content with that opening panel. Since the

Peter and John were arrested in the temple	Paul was arrested in the temple
Peter and John were imprisoned	Paul was imprisoned
Peter and John appeared before the High Priest and the Sanhedrin	Paul appeared before the High Priest and the Sanhedrin
Peter and John encountered Sadducees	Paul encountered Sadducees

Table 9.2

story has moved back to Jerusalem, Luke shows us that Paul is handled in the typical way the leaders there handled all prominent Christians. Patterns such as these doublets convince me that Luke is closing his book, and that we should not think of the ending as downbeat at all.

8. Two books

Earlier it was noted (chapter 3, p. 39) that it is possible that the opening of Acts echoes the opening of Luke's Gospel; it is sometimes suggested that the closure does too. It is worth comparing the two 'destination' verses, for instance:

> As the time approached for him to be taken up to heaven, Jesus resolutely set out for Jerusalem.
>
> (Luke 9:51)

Paul decided to go to Jerusalem, passing through Macedonia and Achaia. 'After I have been there,' he said, 'I must visit Rome also.' (Acts 19:21)

Here there are two different destinations (heaven and Rome), but the routes to them go through the same place, Jerusalem. Both Jesus and Paul are resolute in their plans, and both journeys are critical: for the existence of the gospel in the first case and for the expansion of the gospel in the second. Each is clearly central to the plot line of its book.

This is where guesswork takes over, and ideas are merely tried out to see if they are plausible. What if the sorrow that accompanied the final journey of Paul echoed the sorrow that accompanied that of Jesus? Could the sermon to the Ephesian elders have been placed there to echo the final discourse of Jesus to his disciples? Could Paul's trials be a shadow of Jesus' trials? The charges against Jesus – that 'We have found this man subverting our nation. He opposes payment of taxes to Caesar and claims to be Christ, a king' (Luke 23:2) – are certainly resonant.

If those kind of echoes seem plausible, might it be the case that the reason for the long shipwreck story is not merely that it happened and Luke was caught up in it, nor that it was expected at this stage in a travel narrative, but that it is a kind of Passion narrative? This is the kind of suffering that Paul was warned about as integral to his apostolic calling (9:15), and integral to the gospel call (1:8; 14:22).

9. The end

As has been said above, this is the definite and intended end of the story. It is not, of course, the end of the story for Paul or Peter, and Luke has not been writing the History of the Early Church, nor even the Acts of the Apostles. Luke wrote volume 2 of the Life and Teaching of Jesus the Christ, crucified, risen, ascended, reigning and returning. Volume 1 showed him come from heaven to Nazareth, then through Jerusalem, back to heaven again. Volume 2 has seen him orchestrate, from heaven, the gospel spread from Jerusalem to Rome. There is nothing more Luke has to tell us; we know all we need to know.

Part III: Preaching Acts

10 | Preaching Acts

This part of the book tries to show how the ways of thinking about Acts that have been outlined contribute to preaching Acts in normal talks and sermons. This is a huge risk, because I have to peek out from behind the guise of a neutral commentator and confess to being a real preacher of real sermons. And here some of them are; which means every other preacher who reads the book will say, 'He did it like *that*?' To which the answer is, 'Yes, I did'; because these are all genuine sermons that have been preached in real churches. In consequence they read very much as they were spoken, although I have had to take out obvious local references and time-bound observations. It has been said that every sermon has a date and an address; I could tell from my notes when I preached them, to whom, what was happening in the church and why. I have tried not to make that too obvious.

Illustrations date very quickly; that is why I tend to use them rarely and, when I do, to remove them later. The consequence is that all these sermons would need some 'warming up' before they could be used again with a new date and address. They are very condensed.

The important point to note, however, is that they are all genuine sermons, which were given with no thought of publication at all. So these are not classroom models, perfectly designed to show the principles at work, but rather street-level evidence of how someone who thinks about Acts in the way I do will try to communicate it. Use them for target practice if you like, but be warned if you preach them: I once preached a sermon series originated by a well-known preacher with a distinctive voice, and *I developed his accent for two months*.

Beginning at the beginning

There are occasional 'sermon notes' in boxes running through these sermons. They are designed to function as a commentary on the reasons for preaching in particular ways and the kinds of choices that preachers have to make as communicators. One frequently repeated box, however, occurs at the beginning of the sermons and has to do with how sermons start.

I currently teach in a theological college, and if I start a sermon with the words 'Please turn to Zechariah 2' there is an audible murmur of pleasure which runs through the congregation in chapel. That has not been my experience in the churches where I have worked or been a member. Most people's world is a long way from the thoughts of the biblical writers, and our task as preachers is to shorten that distance. The introduction is the place where we usually do it, but the process is often cut short and does not work. The reason is that we have the wrong model for what we are trying to do.

Model 1 gives a light-hearted introduction, usually about a recent sporting or television event, and, with a simple 'You know, our passage talks about something like that', springs neatly across the bridge. The reason it does not work is that the comparison is inevitably false.

Model 2 dives straight into the text, but with an expectation that people will be interested in the grammatical context. This is, of course, what fascinates the Bible teacher, but it rarely fascinates the average Christian from the outset, although when they have been shown *why* it is significant they will pay close attention.

Model 3 assumes that the Bible text is difficult in itself and needs to be made relevant. Underlying this is the picture of a bridge crossing a yawning chasm, with the Bible on one side in its world or worlds, the twenty-first-century world on the other and the preacher trying to communicate the timeless principles across the bridge to time and culture.

There are several worrying features of this model. First, it must assume that the Bible becomes increasingly difficult to understand the longer we exist. Secondly, it must assume that the Bible is not relevant in itself. Thirdly, it must assume that some of the things the Bible found relevant we no longer do. Fourthly, it must assume that there are some things which we find relevant but which the Bible does not address. Fifthly, it must assume that the gap between then and now is much greater than the gap between, say, Jerusalem and Caesarea, or between Ephesus and Rome, and that the common relevance they shared will find no echo today.

Underlying all these assumptions lies, I think, a faulty view of God. Peter Adam, in *Speaking God's Words*,[1] has correctly drawn attention to the biblical view of inspiration, which is that what God said then, to the biblical readers, he also intended to say now, to us. Rather than moving directly from the Bible to the contemporary world, we travel via the original readers and then (if they were Old Testament readers) through the gospel. Adam helpfully depicts it like this:[2]

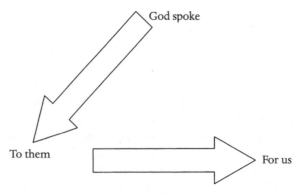

Figure 10.1

---

1. Leicester: Inter Varsity Press (1996).

2. P. 100.

That 'for us' is significant, because a tremendous amount hangs on what we put there. At the least, it will mean Christians. More particularly, it might mean every conceivable opportunity for the passage to be studied. Or, more particularly still, it could well mean, in God's infinite wisdom, every actual time that the passage would be studied, foreseen and foreknown. Is that a likely implication of the Bible's view of God? I think it is. The God who has been at work in Acts, for instance, is the one who has carefully nurtured the churches down every path they need to take, and nothing has happened outside his sovereign will.

If that is true, a radical principle emerges. There is *no great gap* to be bridged, because *God had this Sunday, this congregation and this sermon in mind* when he inspired the original passage. In that case we need never worry about making the Bible relevant. It *is* relevant, because of the character of the God who inspired it, and has particular relevance every time we open it.[3]

What has this to do with the introduction? On a simple level, introduce the issue you are going to be talking about, rather than simply the passage you are going to be talking about. You will at some stage need to introduce the passage, and you may decide that the introduction is the place to do it. But if the Bible is relevant and addresses some issue in the church today (which it always will, because it shares God's character as his word), begin with the issue it will address. Begin with the doubt the promise defeats, or the question it answers, or the idol it smashes, or the lie it unmasks. Subvert. Begin with the application or implication of the section that you will be driving towards with every point and sub-point. You will not need to move out of the Bible's world to speak to our world, because *the Bible's world is our world*; it's God's world, which he addresses in his word.

I have, then, not provided many introductions, because their function was to make sure that *this* congregation was ready to hear God speak on *this* occasion. But I have given indications of how I might think about drawing them up. And if you do happen to have

---

3. For a thorough defence of God's sovereignty with regard to his word, see Vern Poythress, *God-Centered Biblical Interpretation* (Phillipsburg: Presbyterian and Reformed, 1999), especially chapter 9.

a congregation which murmurs in anticipation when you announce a sermon on Zechariah 2, don't give in to it. You are not speaking about Zechariah 2 – you are speaking in the name of the living God. 'Be still before the LORD, all mankind, because he has roused himself from his holy dwelling' (Zech. 2:13).

11 | The most important person in the world – No question: 2:1–39

Preaching note

There are two different ways to handle the evangelistic sermons in Acts. One is to teach the content to both Christians and non-Christians simultaneously, which is what I have tried to do here, and only at the end to address the non-Christians present directly. We should remember that Peter's Pentecost sermon is primarily not a talk about the Holy Spirit to Christians, but a talk about Jesus to non-Christians.

The second way is to recognize that there are two potential audiences, who listen in different ways and with different questions. In the sermons on Acts 10 (chapter 13) I have tried to show how we can separate the two audiences with two different talks.

A preacher will need to able to select which is the most appropriate model to adopt given the particular event being spoken at.

Introduction

See 'Beginning at the beginning' (pp. 117–120)

It was a day of many remarkable events, of course, especially people speaking in foreign languages which they had never learned; that was a major miracle which Jesus had never done before. Luke lists fifteen languages in simultaneous translation in verse 12. And that is not the most remarkable event of all.

It's remarkable that God pours out his Spirit on all people

'In the last days, God says, I will pour out my Spirit on all people' (v. 17). Joel's message, which Peter says is being fulfilled, is one of judgment – and then of hope beyond judgment. It's an odd quotation at first sight, because Joel doesn't talk about tongues, but about 'blood and fire and billows of smoke. The sun will be turned to darkness and the moon to blood' (vv. 19–20), and those sorts of things don't seem to be happening in Acts 2. But Peter is insistent that 'this is what was spoken by the prophet Joel' (v. 16), and that's because Joel's language is typical Old Testament language for the end of history, which is when he understands these things will occur. There are three blessings he points out.

The pouring out of God's Spirit will lead to new understanding, because of the 'visions', 'dreams' and people who will 'prophesy'. When God spoke in the Old Testament it was to say what he was like, what his expectations and promises were. Peter is saying that there is a new era in God's revelation: a new understanding of his plan that has come with the gift of the Holy Spirit.

The pouring out of God's Spirit will lead to new possibilities, because the Spirit will come on 'all people'. In the Old Testament the Spirit came on prophets and kings: the leaders of the nation. In this new era, he comes to all kinds of people (not just the leaders) and to all nations of people (not just Israel).

The pouring out of God's Spirit will lead to a new future, marked by that extraordinary sequence of 'blood . . . fire . . . smoke . . . darkness' and the 'moon' turning to 'blood'. This sounds – and is *meant* to sound – like the end of the world; or, as Peter puts it, quoting Joel, these are the 'last days' (v. 17). Jesus' resurrection is so significant that it marked the start of the end of the world: the start of the last days. And so we know what the future holds, and how to prepare for it. That, in part, is what Peter means by our all being prophets.

The conclusion about Jesus is that, because of his death and resurrection, he is the most important person ever in the history of the world. Listen to how Peter puts it, as he moves from Joel to his own day:

'In the last days,' *God says,*
   'I will pour out my Spirit on all people.'
(v. 17)

Exalted to the right hand of God, *he [Jesus]* has received from the Father the promised Holy Spirit *and [he] has poured out* what you now see and hear.
(v. 33)

Because of his death and resurrection, Jesus has taken on God's responsibility to pour out the Spirit, and he now sits on God's throne, in heaven, as God's appointed King. That's the first remarkable event.

It's remarkable that God offers salvation to all people

'Everyone who calls on the name of the Lord will be saved' (v. 21), says Peter. Is the judgment in the Last Days going to be fearful? Yes, says Peter, but there's also the possibility of rescue from the judgment. The Old Testament was clear about that for faithful Jews, but opaque about the Gentiles, although there is often a note of hope. The Day of Pentecost was the day when that all became marvellously clear, for 'there were staying in Jerusalem God-fearing Jews from every nation under heaven' (v. 5), which included 'Parthians, Medes and Elamites; residents of Mesopotamia, Judea and Cappadocia, Pontus and Asia, Phrygia and Pamphylia, Egypt and the parts of Libya near Cyrene; visitors from Rome (both Jews and converts to Judaism); Cretans and Arabs' (vv. 9–11). That's not literally every nation, of course, and Acts will show that Luke knew many others, but it's a great foretaste of what will happen one day.

The conclusion about Jesus is again clear when we hear how Peter moves from Old Testament quotation to his own day.

Everyone who calls
    on *the name of the Lord* will be saved.
(v. 21)

Repent and be baptised, every one of you, *in the name of Jesus Christ* for the
forgiveness of your sins. And you will receive the gift of the Holy Spirit.
(v. 38)

For the second time, Peter takes titles and roles which in the Old
Testament refer to God, and puts them on Jesus: here Jesus becomes
the 'name' by which we must be saved. He is 'the Lord', who sits on
his heavenly throne until he returns to judge.

Why is Jesus so significant? Why does Peter think he has all these titles
heaped upon him? Well, he says, take the greatest king that Jerusalem
ever saw, King David, the founder of the kingdom. Where is he now?
Rotting in his tomb. Or, as Peter puts it, 'Brothers, I can tell you confi-
dently that the patriarch David died and was buried, and his tomb is here
to this day' (v. 29). Which causes a problem for those who notice that
David has said something rather different, apparently about himself:

I saw the Lord always before me.
    Because he is at my right hand,
    I will not be shaken.
Therefore my heart is glad and my tongue rejoices;
    my body also will live in hope,
because you will not abandon me to the grave,
    nor will you let your Holy One see decay.
You have made known to me the paths of life;
    you will fill me with joy in your presence.
(vv. 25–28)

Peter's solution is that David, as well as being a king and a poet, was a
'prophet' (v. 30). 'Seeing what was ahead, [David] spoke of the resurrection of the Christ, that he was not abandoned to the grave, nor
did his body see decay' (v. 31). The one who was raised to life, then,
has to be the 'Christ' (v. 31) and the 'Lord' (v. 25). Or, as Peter summarized it at the end of the sermon, 'God has made this Jesus, whom
you crucified, *both Lord and Christ*' (v. 36).

So what? For Christians

A clear head is needed, because we need to insist, on Pentecost Sunday of all Sundays, that there aren't two gospels – one about Jesus and one about the Spirit – or even three gospels, one about his cross, one about his resurrection and the third about the Spirit. The Holy Spirit is God's gift to us through the risen Jesus, and he is Jesus' gift because of Jesus' death and resurrection. Which is why the heart of Peter's preaching is not about the Spirit at all, but about Jesus. Pentecost is a hugely significant, one-off event, just as Jesus' death and resurrection are one-off events.

A grateful heart is needed, because, whatever our experience of what God does in our lives, we must remember that all our hope is located in Jesus and what God has done through him. Judgment is real, and the rescue is real. It's so obvious, but it is so easily forgotten, that we must keep on saying it.

So what? For people who are not yet Christians

You're in this story too! Remember that on the Day of Pentecost there were only a handful of Christians. Everyone in that vast crowd was in the same position as you, hearing the message and deciding what to do about it. So what does Peter say to you?

First, there is a warning, because 'God has made this Jesus, whom [they] crucified, both Lord and Christ' (v. 36). There is no alternative to meeting Jesus, face to face, and giving him an account of your life. There is no alternative future of eternal light, or blank nothing, or reincarnation. Only Jesus as your judge.

Just think for a moment how that would have gone down with the crowd. Think about Peter's words, 'God has made this Jesus, whom you crucified, both Lord and Christ.' That must have been the worst news imaginable, don't you think? They have just arranged the murder of God's own king – and God has brought him back to life to judge them for it! Is it any wonder that 'When the people heard this, they were cut to the heart and said to Peter and the other apostles, "Brothers, what shall we do?"' (v. 37). That's the bad news, and it is very bad news indeed, but there is good news too.

Second, there is an offer.

Repent and be baptised, every one of you, in the name of Jesus Christ for the forgiveness of your sins. And you will receive the gift of the Holy Spirit. The promise is for you and your children and for all who are far off – for all whom the Lord our God will call.

(vv. 38–39)

Slow that down, and you'll see the offer. Start with the problem, which is *sin*. The Bible's great story is that sin is rebelling against God, refusing to acknowledge his Lordship and running your life your own way. It means ignoring him, despising him, and ultimately – as these people put into action – it means murdering him. *Sin* is serious, because it causes a massive shift in our relationship with God, and means he acts as our Judge. *Sin*, then, takes the form of rebellion and leads to judgment.

And that's the huge crowd on Pentecost Sunday, and it's you too. It's what everyone does. And fortunately for people like us, God won't go away and leave us to our own miserable end. He makes an offer of 'the forgiveness of your sins'. That rebellion, that despising, even that murder of God, can all be removed from our consciences and from God's records. How?

Step one: repent. That is, stop running; stop rebelling; and come back to God as your rightful king. Say you were wrong and that he is right. It's more than saying sorry, although that is the heart of it, because you're not just saying you regret what happened. You are saying you were completely wrong and God is completely right, and if he were to judge you for what you'd done, he would be absolutely just to do so. That is repentance.

Step two: be baptized in the name of King Jesus. That is what the title 'Jesus Christ' means: King Jesus. So someone who is baptized in Jesus' name is moving from rebellion to submission: from denying Jesus' claim to be Lord of your life, to fully surrendering to that claim.

Can you imagine how that went down on Pentecost Day? They had to submit to the very one they had murdered, because God had appointed him as their judge. And that submission doesn't mean grovelling and eating dirt, but discovering that King Jesus says, 'I forgive you; and if I forgive you, there's no-one left to judge you.'

> See 'Finishing an evangelistic talk', after the sermon on Acts 10, 'Everyone *must* become a Christian' (chapter 14, pp. 145–146).

12 | Making good decisions under pressure: 6:1–7

Preaching note: Introduction
The key here is to see that while the early church was under periods of severe external pressure, these alternated, in this section of Acts, with severe internal crises which were potentially just as destructive. Anyone who has been in a church for any time knows that rows about money happen all the time, and we might have observed that under the surface such seemingly trivial disagreements often have an uglier component too. So begin by talking about the church's own experience of pressures, internal and external, and how apparently trivial ones (here seemingly about money) can be enormously damaging, because underneath they are about something else (which here is race). And do it so that you raise the problem for which the passage will give the answer.

The early church in Jerusalem, as the previous part of Acts shows, was going through severe pressure from outside: physical violence, threats and official warnings. And as we watch its members, the key question is, 'Will the pressure stop them preaching? Will it stop them telling people about Jesus?' The answer was a definite 'No'. 'Day after day, in the temple courts and from house to house, they never stopped teaching and proclaiming the good news that Jesus is the Christ' (5:42). Outward pressure had been a strengthening experience, and they had responded well to it.

But this section shows a different sort of pressure: insidious, demoralizing and distracting pressure from other Christians. We'll stop the action in four freeze-frames and watch as the church faced a distracting problem, came up with a principled answer, made an imaginative decision and then took decisive action. Those four freeze-frames will show us how we cope with similar pressures in our church family.

Preaching note

These four freeze-frames are designed to begin in themselves the move to application. Since the passage is not about merely repeating the precise lesson of appointing deacons to serve at tables but a more general line of how the church is to prioritize different aspects of ministry, so the sermon will do the same. I would apply each of those four areas to the congregation as I moved through, rooting it in a decision we were currently facing or had come through.

Face the distracting problem

This, then, is the first church row, and it's over money. At least, it is on the surface.

> 'In those days when the number of disciples was increasing, the Grecian Jews among them complained against the Hebraic Jews because their widows were being overlooked in the daily distribution of food.'
> (6:1)

It's a rather complex little picture, so let me guide you through it. You may remember how generous the early Christians were, and this generosity meant that the poorer members of the church – widows, in this case – were given food and money out of the general fund. The catch was this. At this stage all the Christians were converted Jews: no Gentiles at all. But the Jewish Christians fell into two groups: those who lived in Israel and spoke Aramaic with a bit of Greek, called 'the Hebraic Jews'; and those who had lived in the wider world and spoke Greek as their first language, maybe with a bit of Aramaic, called here the 'Grecian Jews'. So, although the row is over money, the two sides are drawing up on racial lines, and it's starting to look ugly.

To make things worse, the church leaders, the apostles, were all 'Hebraic Jews', coming from Palestine. And the 'Grecian Jews' were feeling that the widows from their camp were doing less well out of the community pot. The apostles were prejudiced – racially prejudiced – and very unfair. The Grecian Jews complain, and their complaint reaches the ears of the apostles, because ultimately it's a complaint against their leadership qualities and Christian standards.

So the twelve gather everyone together and explain the pressure they are under. Now what happens when you are under pressure? You prioritize. Is it more important to write that letter or see that person? Is it more important to get the car in for a service or to get the shopping? And the pressure mounts, because both things are important and yet you have to choose between them. Hence the apostles' dilemma: the charity work is essential for the church, but solving this problem will take time and tact, and that will potentially distract them from their preaching duties.

So the question is the same as in the last section of Acts, but now it's inside the church: will this *internal* pressure stop the gospel being preached? And the answer is the same: 'the Twelve gathered all the disciples together and said, "It would not be right for us to neglect the ministry of the word of God in order to wait on tables."' (6:2).

Come up with a principled answer

That listing of priorities is as much of a hot potato now as it was then, and one that the churches still have problems getting right. Is our social action important? Yes, very. It is essential to our existence as a church that we display God's love in actions, not just words. Is our preaching important? Yes, very. It is essential to our existence as a church that we explain God's love in words, not just actions. Luke even uses the same word to describe these two tasks: behind the word *ministry* in the phrase 'the ministry of the word' lies the same Greek word 'to wait on tables'. One group serves up food, the other serves up Bible teaching. For any individual there are only twenty-four hours in the day: *so which is the priority?*

It has to be, of course, with finding a way to keep that food-aid programme going, but to free the apostles from running it so they can teach and evangelize. And believe me: as any pastor will tell you, and any member of any church committee will tell you, this problem has not gone away. I could fill my diary several times every day with good and worthy things that ought to be done. I could visit every church member every six months, or visit each home in the area whose inhabitants do not come to church; or visit anyone we know isn't with us this morning. That was put to me this week. Someone has to serve on our denominational committees and synods, and the local community health projects; the dilemma hasn't gone. Virtually every week, I have Greeks in one ear and Hebraists in the other! But Peter's answer still seems the most principled and biblically consistent: the preaching and teaching ministry must not suffer through other valid ministry pressures.

The principled solution was careful delegation of key ministries.

Brothers, choose seven men from among you who are known to be full of the Spirit and wisdom. We will turn this responsibility over to them and will give our attention to prayer and the ministry of the word.
(Acts 6:3–4)

In order to free the apostles for their pastoring ministry of preaching, teaching and praying for the people under their care, other people have to take on their own rightful ministries. Those other jobs are just as much ministries as the ones the apostles are engaged in, but they have to be arranged in such a way that the central preaching, teaching and praying don't get squeezed out.

> **Preaching note**
> At this point you might want to outline how your congregation is
> structured to reflect these priorities, even if it is only sketchy. It is
> critical to point out that congregation members are doing these
> things not because the clergy are lazy (although it's worth owning
> up to that, if it's true!), but so that they are able to exercise their
> ministries too, and the pastor teacher's ministry is preserved.

The apostles' decision is also highly flexible: it can meet new needs
and cope with emerging opportunities, and can answer the critical
difficulties right away. We need to make sure, both here and in any
other congregation that we're ever part of, that we're not stuck with
yesterday's method. The crisis in the early church arose precisely
because of a new factor: 'the number of disciples was increasing'
(6:1). Circumstances change, and what works in one time is weak in
another. It ought to sadden us that churches are thought of as bas-
tions of the past, never changing. Of course the *gospel* doesn't
change; but it is in order that the unchanging gospel can be preached
that the apostles instigate change, and the church is happy to have it.
The church does the work of the church, its ministries, and the apostles do the work of the apostles, their ministries.

Make an imaginative decision

Freeze-frame three is their imaginative decision.

> 'Brothers, choose seven men from among you who are known to be full of
> the Spirit and wisdom. We will turn this responsibility over to them and will
> give our attention to prayer and the ministry of the word.' This proposal
> pleased the whole group. They chose Stephen, a man full of faith and of the
> Holy Spirit; also Philip, Procorus, Nicanor, Timon, Parmenas, and Nicolas
> from Antioch, a convert to Judaism.
> (6:3–5)

Synagogues at that time used to have little teams of seven to run the
charity work, but look at the qualifications the apostles require! Our

Bible, along with the Good News Bible, makes it look like two quali-fications, but most make it three: as J. B. Phillips translates it, 'men of good reputation who are both practically and spiritually minded'. And obviously they needed all three. When there's a highly charged public row about money, only well-known people – people who can win trust – will do. It's also vital they have something between their ears, and that they are spiritual, godly Christians. Although this is only an admin task, it is still a *ministry*, and a helpful pagan won't do.

> **Preaching note**
> At the time this sermon was preached, the church was electing its public officers for the next three years, and we were facing a fairly hotly contested election. I urged the congregation to make sure that these three principles guided their voting.

I'm sure we all know of churches where seats on the board of elders are passed down from father to son, where senior church members occupy positions by right of longevity; where a place on the Church Council is a long-service award, a Christian gold watch. Let's make sure we have none of that nonsense here. No power plays or jockeying for position. The role of the twelve apostles and the role of the seven are described equally as 'servanthood' – ministry – and that should guide us.

I wonder if you noticed something else about the names of those seven? 'They chose Philip, Procorus, Nicanor, Timon, Parmenas, and Nicolas from Antioch, a convert to Judaism.' You'd be right to think: those are Greek names, not Hebrew ones. The people who were complaining of the injustice were Greek, and so the seven selected to serve were Greek. This means that the Hebraic Christians must have deliberately voted for Greeks. They voted against their group interest in favour of the interests of the whole. Let's build that into our selection too: we want leaders who will do what the church *as a whole* needs, even though my individual part may lose out in consequence.

Take decisive action

So the men were elected and commissioned. 'They presented these men to the apostles, who prayed and laid their hands on them' (6:6). It is very neat, with the apostles symbolically delegating their authority to the seven. Except that it's too neat. The Good News Bible, the Living Bible, J. B. Phillips, the New English Bible, The Message and the Jerusalem Bible all say much the same. But the Revised Standard Version, King James Version, Revised Version, English Standard Version and New American Standard Version translate it slightly differently. So do most modern scholars. Compare the NIV with the ESV, for instance. The NIV says, 'They presented these men to the apostles, who prayed and laid their hands on them', but the ESV says, 'These they set before the apostles, and they prayed and laid their hands on them.'

The difference looks tiny, but is actually quite radical. If that translation is right, and I think it probably is, it means that it's not just the apostles who lay their hands on the seven and pray for them; it's everyone present. The scholar Edward Schweizer says, 'It would grammatically have to be the whole church.'[1] So this isn't a primitive and decorous ordination service, or the first apostolic succession. Everyone – mums, dads, children, new believers, the squabbling widows, the apostles, everyone – commissioned the seven to their new ministry.

What does it mean? That the idea of a church isn't just a few professionals ruling the roost and everyone else in awed silence at their wisdom. No; everyone is part of church. If some people are set aside for a particular role, everyone is involved in choosing them and commissioning them. And that means no-one can argue with the decision.

Creative pressure. It poses new problems and makes us rethink priorities and structures. Here we found a flexible solution: gifted and qualified people, selected and commissioned by the whole church to keep their priorities clear. And the result? Look at verse 7: 'So the word of God spread. The number of disciples in Jerusalem increased rapidly, and a large number of priests became obedient to the faith.' Let's pray for those who are considering joining our ministry team in the next few weeks.

---

1. *Church Order in the New Testament* (London: SCM, 1961), p. 73, fn. 282; emphasis his.

13 | Everyone *may* become a Christian: 10:1–48

Preaching note
There are two obvious ways to preach Acts chapter 10, and the story of Cornelius' conversion. One is to explain to Christians the implications of what Peter learns about inclusion; the other is to give the straight evangelistic message. The first sermon, 'Everyone *may* become a Christian', obviously does the former, and the second, 'Everyone *must* become a Christian', does the latter.

Introduction
See 'Beginning at the beginning', (pp. 117–120).

The story is often called 'the conversion of Cornelius', and that is accurate because it is the account of how a Roman centurion became a Christian. But it's also a story with the apostle Peter in the spotlight, and we watch him changing his mind over whether someone like Cornelius was allowed to be a Christian. His change of mind is so great that some people have even suggested calling the story 'the conversion of Peter'. And it's certainly true that, without this story, billions of people would not have become Christians. Including me.

To see why this is earth-shattering we need to go to what the Bible teaches is the most fundamental division between human beings: the division of Jew from non-Jew, or Gentile. So critical was this distinction that God insisted that it should be literally woven into the fabric of Israel's culture in the clothes they wore and the houses they lived in. Most famously, it affected – and still affects – the Jewish diet:

> [God said] These are the regulations concerning animals, birds, every living thing that moves in the water and every creature that moves about on the ground. *You must distinguish between the unclean and the clean*, between living creatures that may be eaten and those that may not be eaten.
> (Lev. 11:46–47)

The great division

Many explanations have been given for that distinction between clean and unclean food, including health regulations, a primitive kind of medicine, or a test of obedience. Perhaps the most attractive, though, is the simplest: it taught Israel a critical lesson about separation. Every shopping trip or meal being cooked, every day farming or going to the temple, was surrounded by regulations to separate *this* from *that*, and not to allow them to mix or contaminate. Every minute decision taught the major lesson: keep yourself separate from sin, and do not risk contamination.

That was God's clear word through Moses, but it was never intended as his final word. God promised Moses, and the people through him:

> The LORD said to me: 'What they say is good. *I will raise up for them a prophet like you* from among their brothers; I will put my words in his mouth, and he will tell them everything I command him.'
> (Deut. 18:17–18)

God had a plan and a promise to raise up a second Moses with a message from God, but, as the time wore on, no such prophet came.

> Since then, no prophet has risen in Israel like Moses, whom the Lord knew face to face, who did all those miraculous signs and wonders the Lord sent him to do in Egypt – to Pharaoh and to all his officials and to his whole land. For no-one has ever shown the mighty power or performed the awesome deeds that Moses did in the sight of all Israel.
> (Deut. 34:10)

As the era of the Old Testament closed, such a prophet, accompanied by 'miraculous signs and wonders', was still expected. Which explains the gasp of astonishment which greeted Jesus' words 'If you believed Moses, you would believe me, for he wrote about me' (John 5:46). Jesus was claiming to be on a level with Moses: everything Moses said had stood until he, the one Moses prophesied, arrived, and then everything Moses said could be reworked. And when he does, it is the end of the great division.

The end of the great division

As Jesus addresses this issue of separation and ritual uncleanness, his first word is to lift the food laws.

> 'Are you so dull?' he asked. 'Don't you see that nothing that enters a man from the outside can make him "unclean"? For it doesn't go into his heart but into his stomach, and then out of his body.' (*In saying this, Jesus declared all foods 'clean'.*)
> (Mark 7:18–19)

This is why it is inadequate to see these laws merely as hygienic rules. There had been no great scientific advances that had solved the problems of bugs in pork. *Salmonella* remained *Salmonella*.

But if they are a visual aid of a greater uncleanness, then when Jesus deals with that real pollution, the visual aid is no longer needed. In fact it is unhelpful, because what Jesus taught must apply to all people, and so something that limited the message to the one nation of Israel had to be abolished. The visual aid now undermined the message. But Jesus did not leave it there, because we might misunderstand him. If he declares all *foods* clean, then surely he must declare all *people* clean? Certainly not, he says:

> [Jesus] went on: 'What comes out of a man is what makes him "unclean".
> For from within, out of men's hearts, come evil thoughts, sexual immorality,
> theft, murder, adultery, greed, malice, deceit, lewdness, envy, slander,
> arrogance and folly. *All these evils come from inside and make a man "unclean".'*
> (Mark 7:20–23)

Take a superficial look at someone and you will see their actions; take a deeper look, and you will begin to understand the thought processes that underlie them. But deeper yet lies the human heart, and it is there that the problem of uncleanness begins. It is there your problem of uncleanness begins. Deeper than your behaviour, deeper even than your unconscious thought, lies your heart. And that's why you cannot control your thinking or your behaviour.

That is true whether you are a Jew or Gentile. Whether you've always eaten pork or never eaten pork doesn't matter any more, according to Jesus; it's your *heart* that matters, and it is unclean in his sight.

It is sometimes said that Christians are inconsistent in our approach to the Old Testament laws: those laws forbid both eating shellfish, and sexual immorality. Christians sit loose to the food laws, but are obsessed with the sex laws and surely we are merely picking and choosing whichever laws we like to suit our own preferences and prejudices. Now, it is true that the law does forbid both: the food prohibitions are in Leviticus 11 and the sexual prohibitions in Leviticus 18. But the crucial lesson is that Jesus teases them apart. While he declares all foods 'clean', sexual immorality is still a sign that our hearts are 'unclean'. If that is an inconsistency, it is one that has its origin in Jesus, the prophet whom Moses promised, the one who can teach even more clearly than Moses. And the one who can solve the problem of that unclean heart.

Paul describes the problem and the solution this way in Ephesians 2:11–18:

Therefore, remember that formerly you who are Gentiles by birth and called 'uncircumcised' by those who call themselves 'the circumcision' (that done in the body by the hands of men) – remember that at that time you were *separate* from Christ, *excluded* from citizenship in Israel and *foreigners* to the covenants of the promise, *without hope* and *without God* in the world.
(vv. 11–12)

In a nutshell, those five terms describe the condition of people who break all the Old Testament laws, including those food laws. You can't be more distant from God than that. But that is only the problem, not the solution, as Paul goes on:

But now in Christ Jesus you who once were far away have been brought near through the blood of Christ. For he himself is our peace, who has made the two one and *has destroyed the barrier, the dividing wall of hostility, by abolishing in his flesh the law with its commandments and regulations*. His purpose was to create in himself one new man out of the two, thus making peace, and in this one body to reconcile both of them to God through the cross, by which he put to death their hostility. He came and preached peace to you who were far away and peace to those who were near. For through him we both have access to the Father by one Spirit.
(vv. 13–18)

The law, says Paul, which was designed to teach Israel to be holy and separate and therefore by definition kept Gentiles out, has now been abolished by the death of Christ, because he died to make a way for everyone, Jew or Gentile, to have that deep heart uncleanness forgiven. Now Jew and Gentile can come to God together, on a level standing, through the cross.

That is exactly the vision which Peter had on the rooftop. It wasn't about food – he knew that – but it took the visit from Cornelius' messengers to explain the real meaning. Without Peter's vision, not only Cornelius, but most Christians in history would not have become believers, and Christianity would have remained a Jewish sect. But because of Peter's vision there is a key to world evangelization. Once he had preached this sermon there really was no going back for the gospel, because there are no racial barriers at all to the message once this fundamental barrier has been overcome.

Think about [a country in that day's news]. There are [statistics] Christians in that country. That there are Christians there at all is a marvel of God's grace, because almost everyone there is, like almost everyone here, not Jewish. And yet God in his great kindness has allowed them to become Christians. And if Cornelius had not been converted, that would never have happened. That's how critical this story is.

That means there are [statistics] people who are not Christians in that country. If we lived BC – before Cornelius – we'd say, of course they are not Christians. They are somewhere else believing something else. The gospel is not for *them*; it is for people like *us*. But we do not live BC. We live after these great events, and the result is that there is no-one, anywhere, with any religious background, who does not have the right to have the gospel preached to them. People sometimes say that the era of the missionary is dead. I think, given the billions of people who have never heard about Jesus, and who never will unless someone tells them, like Peter told Cornelius, that the era of the missionary has hardly started.

So it is basic to the Bible that anyone *may* become a Christian. And it is a dreadful thing when churches lock it into a racial, or generational, or social, or class club. And it is to our shame that Christianity in our country is often perceived – rightly – as middle class, white, affluent, ageing and culturally elitist.

Ending

A challenge to involvement in mission, possibly even to changing career for life.

---

14 | Everyone *must* become a Christian: 10:1–48

Preaching note

The second way to preach Acts chapter 10 is to give the straight evangelistic message, which is the pattern here. It is the kind of talk to give at evangelistically organized events such as breakfasts or barbecues, as well as in church. I would have the Bible passage printed out, together with some key bullet points and the response form (see 'Finishing an evangelistic talk', pp. 145–146).

More than with any other of these sermons, these notes form the bare bones of what I said, to show how an evangelistic talk can follow the contours of the message in Acts. They need to be thoroughly warmed up and personalized.

Introduction

See 'Beginning at the beginning' pp. 117–120.

When you think of the least likely people to become Christians, who comes to mind? God chooses for this episode the least likely person imaginable: a thoroughly decent bloke.

Cornelius was a good person

Cornelius was the kind of person you would like as a next-door neighbour. A professional man, Luke says that 'he and all his family were devout and God-fearing; he gave generously to those in need and prayed to God regularly' (10:2). And God knew that about him, because the angel said, 'Your prayers and gifts to the poor have come up as a memorial offering before God' (10:4).

Perhaps you even think that's a bit like you; in which case watch what happens next. Notice what has happened when Cornelius prayed. God answered his prayer by sending a missionary to convert him. He is exactly the kind of person we would think didn't need to become a Christian – a thoroughly decent person with a spiritual dimension – but God thinks that even he needs to become a believer. To do that he needs to hear what he is really like in God's eyes.

An unexpected message of judgment

Peter told Cornelius what you might think is the standard Christian message. I am sure Luke has summarized it for us, but the shape is clear.

In verses 37–39 Peter tells Cornelius about Jesus' life and impact. Peter was speaking at a time when all this could have been checked, and Luke, who wrote it up for us, says he was careful in using his sources. So, all of Jesus' teaching, like the Sermon on the Mount and the Lord's Prayer, all of his miracles and healings, all have a basis in reality and history. Peter is taking a risk here, and he wouldn't have started the conversation unless he knew Jesus was real.

If any of you are working with the idea that Jesus was a fantasy figure like Gandalf, or someone lost in myth like King Arthur, then can I encourage you to take on board the real, historical evidence for Christianity.

> **Preaching note**
> Here I would recommend a book such as *The Case for Christ* by
> Lee Strobel (Zondervan/Harper Collins, 1998), which should be
> on the bookstall, or advertise a course for people with questions.
> See the note below on 'Finishing an evangelistic talk', pp. 145–146.

In verse 39 Peter explains about Jesus' crucifixion. The reference to
Jesus' death 'on a tree' is one of the early Christians' standard ways of
explaining the cross; Luke notes it several times in Acts.[1] It is a reference to a method of execution in the Old Testament, which showed
that the criminal was under God's curse.

The Bible is insistent that when Jesus died he faced God's anger
not for anything that he had done, but for everything we have done.
You and I have twisted right and wrong, lied through our teeth,
borne grudges and a host of other things that God says are just plain
wrong. More than wrong, in fact; they are criminal.

Then in verses 40–41 Peter outlines Jesus' resurrection, together
with some proofs for it. Jesus is, as Peter had said in verse 36, 'Lord of
all'. Peter is quite clear, as an eyewitness, that he didn't see a ghost,
and Jesus didn't have a near-death experience. He met Jesus, alive
after his death.

So what? Well, Peter moves in a most unexpected direction. Jesus 'is
the one whom God appointed as judge of the living and the dead'
(10:42). The central impact of the resurrection is that God has installed
Jesus as the universal *Judge*, and he is the one who finds every one of us
unclean. Even decent Cornelius. Even decent people like you and me.

Fortunately, Peter does not stop there.

An unexpected message of forgiveness

The good news which follows the bad news is that 'all the prophets
testify about him [i.e. Jesus] that everyone who believes in him

---

1. Acts 5.30; 13:29; cf. Deut. 21:23. You might need those references for the
   'Unplugged' session afterwards.

receives forgiveness of sins through his name' (10:43). All the Old Testament prophets, the ones we normally think of as the gloom-and-thunder merchants, were busily telling people that the future held the promise of forgiveness and a way out of the uncleanness the law exposed. And the way out, underlined three times by Peter here, is through Jesus.

So Jesus is both the judge and the forgiver; the one who says Cornelius is unclean and the one who died to make him clean. So – and this is a fantastic moment in world history – Cornelius becomes a believer. And not only did Peter tell Cornelius about Jesus' acts of 'power' (10:38), proving he was the great prophet; Cornelius' conversion was accompanied by the miraculous gift of speaking other languages, a mark of how significant this event was in God's plan.

To become personal for a minute, that means two things are true for everyone here today. The first is that you *can* become a Christian. It doesn't matter how bad you are, or what you've done; everything about you is summed up in that one word 'unclean'. That's Jesus' word for us, and if you're looking into your heart and find yourself agreeing, and saying 'Yes, that's how I see myself too', the fantastic news is that the forgiveness Cornelius found can be yours too. I'm going to pray a simple prayer in a moment, and you can join in with me. I've printed it out on the sheet with the Bible passage.

> **Preaching note**
> On this prayer and the sheet, see below, p. 146.

The second truth is that you *must* become a Christian, because otherwise your future is alarming. You will meet Jesus, because he is 'Judge of the living and the dead' (10:42), and you already know what his verdict on you is. You might be as decent, generous and religious as Cornelius – but remember, he had to become a Christian. And if decent people like him need to become Christians, then decent people like you need to become Christians too. Because you, too, are *unclean*. Your behaviour shows it, your thoughts show it, and your heart knows it too. So that prayer on the sheet is for you too. Let me talk you through it.

Preaching note: Finishing an evangelistic talk
The best advice on this is contained in *Setting Hearts on Fire* by John Chapman (Kingsford, NSW: Matthias Media, 1999). Put simply, the goal is to avoid manipulation, but to make accepting Christ an unembarrassing thing to do. So the sheet should have the Bible passage on it, with the outline for your talk, so people know where you are heading. It should also have some prayer of commitment, so people know what they are signing up to. There needs to be space for name, address, e-mail and so on. And I put the four letters A, B, C, and D. You also want to make sure that people have some way of filling in the sheet, so make sure there are pens available. I finish an evangelistic talk on these lines:

I find that as I give talks like this there are four kinds of responses, and you might find it helpful to grab a pen and put a ring round the letter that most feels like you.

A stands for 'Absolutely. I agree with every word you've said, and have done for a number of years.' That's great, and if you really agreed with every word, thank you for not falling asleep, or for not snoring if you did.

D is at the other end of the scale, and it stands for 'Don't believe a word of it.' Again, thank you for not falling asleep or snoring – and thank you too for not disagreeing out loud with me! I would say, though, that the evidence for Jesus is so strong that the only way you can disagree with everything I've said is to ignore some pretty plain facts and distort the data. But you can grab me to tackle that if you want. *[Note: maybe you could think about having an 'unplugged' session after an evangelistic talk, where you could handle questions in a more informal way? Notice how I've tried to provoke this person so they would hang on for such an event.]* There's space on the back of the sheet if you want to give me some feedback.

C stands for 'Considering it. I'm not saying you're wrong and I'm not saying you're right, but I'm open-minded.' If that's you, then I've some things to recommend. One is the book you can get at the back over coffee, which I mentioned earlier. The second is our course, which looks at Jesus on his own terms and reads one of the four gospels together. And the third is a group we have starting in a couple of weeks' time, where we're going to look at why God allows suffering; other religions; all the kinds of questions that people have buzzing round their heads. *[Note: this*

'C' group will be much larger than the 'D' group, because the "D" group by and large won't have come! So give lots of different opportunities for people to examine the truth-claims of Christianity, and to have their genuine questions answered.]

B stands for 'Beginning tonight, I've decided I need to stop running away from God, and turn my life over to him.' That's the best news of all, and if that's you, have a look at that prayer on the sheet again. It simply acknowledges God's right to run your life, says you are sorry for rebelling against him, thanks him for Jesus' death in your place to take your place, and commits you to following Jesus in the future. Would you like to pray that prayer with me?

. . . If you did pray that prayer, your life has now changed. You are, no matter what you've done, 'clean'. Now that takes time to sink in, so if you take that sheet to the welcome table at the back you'll find some friendly people who'll give you a cup of coffee, and a copy of this talk and another one called 'How to know I've become a Christian'. That's all – no pressure, no manipulation. And if you want to, put your name and address on the sheet and I'll drop you a line later this week.

[Note: unless you have very good recording equipment, you'd better have recorded the tape of this talk beforehand! But have it, and the other one on Assurance, available in several formats. Make sure there are friendly people and coffee around, and some adverts for your follow-up course. Remember: conversion is God's job, not yours, and you don't need any high-pressure techniques to convert people. What you do need, however, is the courage to ask the question 'Would you like to pray that prayer right now?']

15 | Why intelligent people can also be stupid: 17:16–31

Preaching note
The goal of the first half of this sermon is for people to get inside the mind of someone who admired the first-century Greek world, so that they then experience the force of Paul's critique from the inside. It is not aimed at non-Christians (although it has an evangelistic edge at the end), but Acts 17 should be preached evangelistically as well.

Introduction
See 'Beginning at the beginning', (pp. 117–120).

Henry lived a secret life. By day he was quite respectable: he worked in a firm of local solicitors, paid his taxes and went to church. He was faithful to his wife and a good dad.

But by night, Henry became a man obsessed: hours spent in the local library, hundreds of pounds spent on books and videos. Henry was a different man, because he had a secret love: Ancient Greece.

Whenever he could grab a free day he'd be visiting the British Museum; the Ashmolean; anything to feed his craving. And one day, he vowed, he'd go. Not to tourist Greece, with the beaches and tavernas, which is where the boys wanted to be, but to archaeologists' Greece: ruins and statues. One day, when the boys were old enough to go on holiday by themselves, he and his wife would go to Greece, and he'd have two weeks among the ruins, dreaming.

It didn't happen for a number of years, and in the end his wife didn't fancy the kind of dusty trip he had in mind, but he went, by himself. He drank in everything he could see: the Parthenon and the little temples, the statues and the theatres. He paced round hardly-visible sites with a guidebook that began to fall apart. He stood on the Acropolis and tried to imagine what it looked like all that time ago, with the priests, the processions, the incense and the sacrifices. He tried to grasp the overwhelming majesty of it all.

Now Henry was English, and emotions were deeply foreign to him, but he even began to feel a little tickle at the back of his throat; a little sniff in the nose; a little blurring in his eyes. The whole trip was proving to be deeply moving for him. He thought of the insights into truth that the ancient Greeks had, and that we'd lost. He thought of the wonderful beauty of their society and the ugliness of ours. And Henry began to wish he had been a Greek.

The apostle Paul was a tourist in Greece too, and a long ambition was met as he stood on the Acropolis. And as he looked at the beauty and the art, the statues and the little temples, he too was deeply moved. But he wasn't moved by wonder or envy – he was deeply distressed. The opening verse of the reading shows how upset he was: 'While Paul was waiting for them in Athens, he was greatly distressed to see that the city was full of idols' (v. 16). If you have visited the British Museum in London you'll have seen the Elgin Marbles, one of the massive friezes from the Parthenon. It is an exquisite marvel of craftsmanship, and it is exactly the kind of idol that so 'distressed' Paul. It is a great religious and artistic triumph, from a peak of human civilization, the Acropolis, and Paul calls it, in verse 30, 'ignorance'.

Any other tourist to Athens might be amazed, with Henry, at the fabulous treasures. But Paul thought it was 'full of idols': swamped with them; stuffed with them. Those wonderful carvings and buildings were foolish religious bric-à-brac.

It is the kind of religious viewpoint that has given Christianity a bad name for religious bigotry. Rather than celebrate their religious culture, Paul calls it anti-God; rather than celebrate their philosophy, he calls it ignorance. Christians today might urge Paul to have a much broader view of religious art. Virtually every cathedral is an artwork in its own right and hosts art exhibitions. Virtually every church is designed to be beautiful, and many contain paintings or statues. In a deep irony, many churches are designed on principles first laid down by the ancient Greeks. We are, surely, much broader than Paul.

We need to hear what Paul says before we dismiss him. When he accuses them of 'ignorance', he is not saying that the intellectual Athenians knew nothing at all, and he will later quote one of their own poets back at them. He means that they are foolish – or, to put it bluntly, stupid – because they don't see what their own eyes should tell them. And he shows them three reasons for his criticism.

Reason 1

People are stupid because they should know the creator of the universe does not live in buildings, but they still act as if he did. Verse 24 puts it clearly: 'The God who made the world and everything in it is the Lord of heaven and earth and does not live in temples built by hands.' How can the God who made everything there is be confined to a stone home? The very idea is absurd.

And yet, people act as if he did! All over Greece, and all over the world, people built and build places where at some level they think God lives, and to show their respect they whisper when they go in. Christians even collude with this: some by calling their buildings 'the house of God', and others by giving some parts of the building special prominence by height or lighting or acoustics to show where the really holy place is.

Paul knew that the only building that God had ever said he had inhabited was the temple in Jerusalem, and that had been a temple which God designed, which had been the dwelling place for his name only, and which he had abandoned when he chose.

Christians ought to know better, and Paul reckoned that the Athenians were intelligent enough to know better too.

Reason 2

People are stupid because they should know that the God who sustains them does not need their care, but they still act as if he did. At this place and time, they would dress the statues in different clothes, as if God needed help with his wardrobe, scoffs Paul. They would leave dishes of food out for the gods to eat. It is not difficult to see examples of this kind of behaviour in religions today, and in Christian churches today too.

And the irony is, we are the ones living in a place God has built for us, and we are the ones whose daily survival depends on the food and air that God gives us. As Paul puts it:

> The God who made the world and everything in it is the Lord of heaven and earth and does not live in temples built by hands. And he is not served by human hands, as if he needed anything, because he himself gives all men life and breath and everything else.
>
> (vv. 24–25)

Do you see how easy it is for intelligent and religious people to be very, very stupid?

Reason 3

People are stupid because they should know that the God who made us must be infinitely greater than us, but they still reduce him to a statue.

Look at verse 29: 'Therefore since we are God's offspring, we should not think that the divine being is like gold or silver or stone – an image made by man's design and skill.' Sometimes when the Bible refers to a religious practice it condemns it outright: human sacrifice, for instance, or cult prostitution. But there is one kind of behaviour for which the Bible's response is often simply mockery, and that is making statues, or painting pictures, of God. Here, for instance, is Isaiah:

> All who make idols are nothing,
> and the things they treasure are worthless.
> Those who would speak up for them are blind;
> they are ignorant, to their own shame.
> Who shapes a god and casts an idol,

which can profit him nothing?
He and his kind will be put to shame;
    craftsmen are nothing but men.
Let them all come together and take their stand;
    they will be brought down to terror and infamy.

The blacksmith takes a tool
    and works with it in the coals;
he shapes an idol with hammers,
    he forges it with the might of his arm.
He gets hungry and loses his strength;
    he drinks no water and grows faint.
The carpenter measures with a line
    and makes an outline with a marker;
he roughs it out with chisels
    and marks it with compasses.
He shapes it in the form of man,
    of man in all his glory,
    that it may dwell in a shrine.
He cut down cedars,
    or perhaps took a cypress or oak.
He let it grow among the trees of the forest,
    or planted a pine, and the rain made it grow.
It is man's fuel for burning;
    some of it he takes and warms himself,
    he kindles a fire and bakes bread.
But he also fashions a god and worships it;
    he makes an idol and bows down to it.
Half of the wood he burns in the fire;
    over it he prepares his meal,
    he roasts his meat and eats his fill.
He also warms himself and says,
    'Ah! I am warm; I see the fire.'
From the rest he makes a god, his idol;
    he bows down to it and worships.
He prays to it and says,
    'Save me; you are my god.'
They know nothing, they understand nothing;

their eyes are plastered over so they cannot see,
and their minds closed so they cannot understand.
No-one stops to think,
no one has the knowledge or understanding to say,
'Half of it I used for fuel;
I even baked bread over its coals,
I roasted meat and I ate.
Shall I make a detestable thing from what is left?
Shall I bow down to a block of wood?'
He feeds on ashes, a deluded heart misleads him;
he cannot save himself, or say,
Is not this thing in my right hand a lie?'
(Isa. 44:9–20)

The irony is withering. Or take Jeremiah's words from God:

'Do not learn the ways of the nations
or be terrified by signs in the sky,
though the nations are terrified by them.
For the customs of the peoples are worthless;
they cut a tree out of the forest,
and a craftsman shapes it with his chisel.
They adorn it with silver and gold;
they fasten it with hammer and nails
so that it will not totter.
Like a scarecrow in a melon patch,
their idols cannot speak;
they must be carried
because they cannot walk.
Do not fear them;
they can do no harm
nor can they do any good.
(Jer. 10:2–5)

Idols, statues – those are great religious works of art being denounced here, made with great feeling and beauty. But they are 'nothing' and 'worthless', and those who speak for them are 'ignorant' (Isa. 44:9) They are so powerless that they have to have others to speak for them; so powerless that they have to have others carry them; so powerless they have to be nailed down to stop them toppling over. That can't be what God is like, can it? And the idol makers say: no, that is not what God is really like. But still they do it, because a powerless god is one you can control and speak for; a powerless god makes people gods in its place.

What is the problem with all this religious jumble? Very simple, says Paul; we made it. They are 'temples built by hands' (v. 24) and statues 'served by human hands' (v. 25) and 'made by man's design and skill' (v. 29). We made all these things, and therefore they can only be idols and cannot be the true God, the *living* God.

Remember Henry? Henry is still at the Acropolis, and he is in tears now, because he has remembered this speech of Paul's. Is Paul saying that the ancient Greeks knew *nothing* about God? That the Ancient Egyptians and Japanese, and today's Buddhists, Muslims and Hindus know *nothing* about God? Nothing at all?

Not at all, says Paul, if we look at him carefully. He says that they know – or ought to know – five facts about the goodness of God, and they should be obvious to even the most persistent idol maker.

The Good God is a Creator God

He made everything. 'The God who made the world and everything in it is the Lord of heaven and earth' (v. 24). So the marble that the sculptor carves, the gold the metalworker shapes, the wood the carpenter turns, the lapis lazuli the painter puts on, the saffron that dyes the thread the embroiderer uses: everything that the artist uses has already been made by God. Our world yells that it has been made by God.

The Good God is a Caring God

'He himself gives all men life and breath and everything else' (v. 25). God has given a great gift to everyone: breath. Life. Consciousness. It is a good thing to be alive, and it is God's continual gift to us.

The Good God is a Controlling God

'From one man he made every nation of men, that they should inhabit the whole earth; and he determined the times set for them and the exact places where they should live' (v. 26). Greeks, and Athenians in particular, thought of themselves as the inheritors of destiny, the ones who could mould the world. People often have the same thoughts today, and Paul reminds us that we are as much the results of accidents and circumstances as any other nation – and that behind those accidents and circumstances stands a God worthy of the name. No nation invents its borders; God gave them, and will take them away.

The Good God is a Close God

> God did this so that men would seek him and perhaps reach out for him and find him, though he is not far from each one of us. 'For in him we live and move and have our being.' As some of your own poets have said, 'We are his offspring.'
> (vv. 27–28)

The intellectual philosopher and thinker may picture God as a remote theory, but the ordinary person, like Paul's poet here, is still basically religious, still prays and still thinks there's a God who cares and is involved.

The Good God is a Compassionate God

If God were an automatic dispenser of justice he would have judged Athens long ago, but throughout the city's long history he 'overlooked such ignorance' (v. 30). And that shows his patience and his desire for a return to a right relationship with him.

So, despite our idol-making hearts, we ought to recognize that God is creating, caring, controlling, close and compassionate.

The Known God

But Paul began his sermon not by talking about what people know about God, but about what they do not know about him. His way in was to talk about, and to explain, the Unknown God. If all those five facts were observably true, what was the unknown part? Simply this.

> In the past God overlooked such ignorance, but now he commands all people everywhere to repent. For he has set a day when he will judge the world with justice by the man he has appointed. He has given proof of this to all men by raising him from the dead.
>
> (vv. 30–31)

What no human ingenuity can work out, what people have to tell others, is that it is the risen Jesus who will be their judge. The risen Jesus is the unknown God.

It is not bigoted of God to tie everything to Jesus like this – it is the reverse. It is wonderfully kind of him to tell us the future, explain what he will do, and explain what the place of Jesus is in it. That is all that Paul wanted to talk about, and how the whole sermon began. Remember how it began?

> While Paul was waiting for them in Athens, he was greatly distressed to see that the city was full of idols. So he reasoned in the synagogue with the Jews and the God-fearing Greeks, as well as in the marketplace day by day with those who happened to be there. A group of Epicurean and Stoic philosophers began to dispute with him. Some of them asked, 'What is this babbler trying to say?' Others remarked, 'He seems to be advocating foreign gods.' They said this because Paul was preaching the good news about Jesus and the resurrection. Then they took him and brought him to a meeting of the Areopagus, where they said to him, 'May we know what this new teaching is that you are presenting? You are bringing some strange ideas to our ears, and we want to know what they mean.' (All the Athenians and the foreigners who lived there spent their time doing nothing but talking about and listening to the latest ideas.)
>
> (vv. 18–21)

The counterweight to all the human ignorance about God is the resurrection of Jesus, which proves (v. 31) that this is what God is like.

So what should you and I do? Well, that depends. It depends on whether you're a Christian or not. Look at verse 30 again. 'In the past God overlooked such ignorance, but now he commands all people everywhere to repent.' If you're not yet a Christian, I would have thought that's a clear instruction, although it is one you will want to think hard about. God *commands* you to turn from your stupidity and serve Jesus. He is not inviting you, or wooing you, or persuading you, here – although he can do that. But here, today, God is ordering you to stop being so stupid. You might find blunt talk like that offensive, and it is not the normal way people talk in church. But it is the blunt talk of the sailor who thrusts a life-jacket at you and tells you – orders you – to jump into the lifeboat.

Preaching note

I would not want to soften the impact of this command by talking too long; but elsewhere in the service I would offer enquirers some leaflet or course and make it known I was available to chat afterwards – maybe do an informal 'Question Time' over coffee.

And if you are a Christian already? Well, I guess we have to join in Paul's chorus, don't we? We have to learn to see the world through God's eyes, not the tourist's brochures. Are you with Paul or Henry? Are you lost in wonder, and have your breath taken away by the holiness of beauty? That's Henry. Or are you distressed that the beauty and experience are actually lies? That's Paul. And it means being committed to telling our ignorant world about the risen Jesus.

We would all love to be able to grab the microphone and, just once, tell the people who run things what they really ought to know. Haven't you had that dream? This time, it's you speaking in the House of Commons to awed silence; it's you addressing that major conference; it's you telling those people who write the policy manual that you have to abide by how they ought to have written it if they'd bothered to ask you in the first place.

Perhaps you even have the speech ready. There's a cartoon of a clergyman in a dressing-gown addressing his bathroom mirror: 'It comes as a complete surprise to be asked to address this Synod.' Maybe it's just the clergyman's version of the dream, but haven't you ever wanted to tell the people who run the church what they ought to be doing? I wonder what you'd say?

Paul had the chance, and he took it. Straight from the shoulder, he told a bunch of church leaders what they really ought to know. These were close friends whom he expected never to see again, and he made a highly emotional speech.

Preaching note

At this point you can link up with previous sermons in the series and bring people up to speed with the context in Acts. But notice: the sermon does not start there. Context is critical for correct exegesis, but the sermon is not about the context; it's about issues for Christian leadership, so it must start with that issue, not with a PowerPoint presentation with maps of Paul's missionary journeys. That information has a place, but not, in my view, at the start of the sermon.

So I would headline two or three issues that are current in the secular press where the church is not faring particularly well and get the listeners to think how they would solve the underlying problem. The aim is to get people who are not church leaders to think themselves into the position of church leaders, so they can feel the force of the message. Then you can move into the text.

Paul started, as we would expect, by remembering. He reminds them of what he had done with them over the previous three years.

> You know how I lived the whole time I was with you, from the first day I came into the province of Asia. I served the Lord with great humility and with tears, although I was severely tested by the plots of the Jews. You know that I have not hesitated to preach anything that would be helpful to you but have taught you publicly and from house to house.
>
> (20:18–20)

This is what the previous section has shown: Paul's ordinary strategy for evangelism. And we see here that his description matches what occurred. His method was teaching 'publicly and from house to house'. He would go where the non-Christians were, speak their language and put things in ways they could understand. That was his method, and it can be summed up as massive flexibility. He would not support any tradition that stood in the way of people hearing about Jesus. He became, as he reminded the Corinthians:

> like a Jew, to win the Jews. To those under the law I became like one under the law (though I myself am not under the law), so as to win those under the

law. To those not having the law I became like one not having the law (though I am not free from God's law but am under Christ's law), so as to win those not having the law. To the weak I became weak, to win the weak. I have become all things to all men so that by all possible means I might save some.

(1 Cor. 9:20–22)

That's massive flexibility, at some personal cost.

Alongside that went the message. 'I have declared to both Jews and Greeks that they must turn to God in repentance and have faith in our Lord Jesus' (20:21). *Both* Jews *and* Greeks: two groups, reached in two different ways with the same message of repentance and faith. And this part of his strategy, his message, is an example of massive *in*flexibility. Flexible in his method; inflexible in his message.

So Paul and the elders reminisce, although of course it's more than merely gazing over old snapshots and remembering how things used to be. He is reminding them in order to drill into them that they must share those same two character traits. He's reminding them of what they heard from him and saw in him, a pattern of ministry that they will follow after he has gone. Through three years which included a riot, trips overseas, an attempted abduction and the wonder of a young man being raised from the dead, Paul can still call them to witness that he has stuck firm to his strategy.

'And now, compelled by the Spirit, I am going to Jerusalem, not knowing what will happen to me there. I only know that in every city the Holy Spirit warns me that prison and hardships are facing me' (Acts 20:22–23). This farewell gives us the reason for his speech, and it is the only time in Acts where we know what Paul said when he addressed Christians, and especially Christian leaders. Luke has told his readers a number of times that Paul said farewell and strengthened the churches, so this must be his typical message, his final charge. As far as the Ephesians were concerned, these were his famous last words.

What would you expect him to say? He's been there three years, remember, building up the church from nothing. Each one of these people has received personal instruction and discipling from Paul himself.

More than that, they are the leaders of the church. They are called 'elders' in verse 17, and it's clear from 1 Timothy 5 that elders were primarily the teachers in the churches. He calls them 'overseers' in verse 28. We might translate that as 'supervisor', and it became common much later to translate it as 'bishop', but that's a touch misleading in today's understanding of the word. These are local church supervisors. And, again in 1 Timothy, such people are to be 'able to teach' (1 Tim. 3:2). In verse 28 he calls them 'shepherds' over a 'flock' and that is Old Testament language for the rulers and leaders of God's people: their kings. The equivalent word in church circles today is 'pastors'. So these people Paul is addressing are the church leaders, or more specifically the church *teachers*.

So Paul has his handpicked team, of whom he can say in verse 28 'the Holy Spirit has made you overseers'. What would you expect him to tell them? 'I know the gifts God has given you, and he will bless your ministries and make your churches grow. I have seen many of you come to faith myself – I have watched you grow and exercise your first steps as teachers here in Ephesus. We believe in a great God – and God will do great things through you.' Does that sound about right? Not a bit of it.

> Keep watch over yourselves and all the flock of which the Holy Spirit has made you overseers. Be shepherds of the church of God, which he bought with his own blood. I know that after I leave, savage wolves will come in among you and will not spare the flock. Even from your own number men will arise and distort the truth in order to draw away disciples after them. So be on your guard! Remember that for three years I never stopped warning each of you night and day with tears.
>
> (20:28–31)

Doesn't that chill your blood? I think it's meant to. Let's take it more slowly – we'll look first at the danger and then at the safe route.

The danger

The danger comes in two parts, first in verse 29 and then in verse 30. Verse 29 has 'savage wolves' coming in to massacre the flock – and remember these men are meant to be the shepherds of that flock.

Who are these wolves? Obviously church wreckers: the ones who come in to mislead and fool the Christians. They might be in it for money or the ego trip, but Paul is desperately concerned that they will arrive almost as soon as he has gone and tear into the flock. 'So how will we recognize a wolf, Paul? Will he wear a helpful badge saying, "I am a wolf, stay away from me"?' Of course not. 'Savage wolves will come in *among you*'. Now remember: he is talking to church leaders here, and they are the people the wolves will come in among in order to devastate the flock. They won't wear a badge saying 'wolf'; it will say 'elder' or 'overseer' or 'pastor'. You've heard of a wolf in sheep's clothing? Well, these are wolves in shepherds' clothing.

Christians today take many things seriously: there are wonderful teaching resources, and there's great music available. We are encouraged to do evangelism well, and there are practical courses available to help us, and there are organizations that will use our money and time to keep the practical arm of the church's programme supported. We take ecumenism seriously, and the arts seriously, and the family seriously, and drugs seriously – and we hardly think to take the danger of heresy seriously. The danger of wolves in shepherds' clothing. And it is a real danger – look at verse 29 – because they do not 'spare the flock', which means that all the other things we do take seriously are ruined. I think if we knew more about farming this image would scare us silly.

Now, of course, if we saw that kind of destruction coming we'd be very careful and avoid it, but these savage animals are very nice people. How else can they slip in unnoticed among the highly trained leadership of Ephesus? Wherever did we get the idea that it would be easy to spot a wolf? This isn't 'Little Red Riding Hood'. This is no fairy tale. Wolves are nice people.

The danger increases with the second part in verse 30. 'Even from your own number men will arise and distort the truth in order to draw away disciples after them.' Be honest: if you didn't have it in black and white in front of you, from Paul's own mouth, would you believe it? Some of his hand-picked, personally trained team of leaders will be people who will pervert the gospel. Does that frighten you? It frightens me – because I am a Bible teacher.

How will you know if I start to 'distort the truth'? Is there a neon light that will flash on the pulpit: 'Please take no further notice of Chris, he has started to spout dangerous drivel'? Of course not. A false teacher will have impeccable credentials, a wonderful manner, and have taught the Bible faithfully for many years. Then suddenly he turns wolfish.

Pray for those of us who preach. Look at our temptation: to 'draw away disciples after' us. It is a very flattering experience to have people politely listening to what I say.[1] Imagine my danger if I started to notice that people came when I spoke on particular topics, but stayed away when I spoke on others. That's the danger here. 'Revd Garry down the road has just started doing X, Y or Z on a Sunday, and he *packs* them in. Perhaps I ought to start doing it too.' It's insidious. Preachers are in a prime position to have their egos stroked, and then they start to preach to win flattery, and then to preach heresy to manipulate people into more flattery, and then they have replaced the Lord Jesus as the teacher of the church, and the flock is being torn to pieces by the wolves.

So please do not underestimate the danger of false teaching. False teaching may teach many different things, do many different things, fake many different things, and take numerous cultural and social forms, but in one aspect it is always identical: it leads to hell. And the flock follows the wolf in sheep's clothing all the way. False teaching is perilous, deadly, poisonous stuff.

The safe route

Is it any wonder that Paul says in verse 28 'Keep watch over yourselves and all the flock of which the Holy Spirit has made you overseers. Be shepherds of the church of God, which he bought with his own blood'? Protect it from others and protect it from you. 'So be on your guard!' (v. 31).

The danger is clear, and Paul's passion about it is clear, but what is the remedy? How, exactly, are they to be on guard and keep watch? We can see it in what Paul was spending his time doing in Ephesus,

---

1. And, of course, read what I have written.

and which he passed on as the model for the elders. During those three years, he said, I taught (v. 20); I declared (v. 21); I testified (v. 24); I preached (v. 25); I proclaimed (v. 27); I warned (v. 31). That was his way of guarding the flock, you see: teaching, teaching, teaching. Teaching what? 'The gospel of God's grace' (v. 24), and 'the word of his grace' (v. 32). In other words, he taught them, over and again, those basic deep truths about God's love for us, our rebellion, Jesus' death for us, and the free forgiveness he has won for us. He taught it time after time, in a hundred different places and thousand different ways, so he can say, 'You know that I have not hesitated to preach anything that would be helpful to you' (v. 20) and 'I have not hesitated to proclaim to you the whole will of God' (v. 27). Those two phrases are even closer than they appear here, because the same Greek word is used for 'preaching' in verse 20 and 'proclaiming' in verse 27.

Do you begin to see the reason for Paul's passion now? For his tears, night and day? For bringing the Ephesian elders almost 30 miles to Miletus? God's people are infinitely precious to him, for 'he bought' us 'with his own blood'. Will Paul sit back and watch those people being ripped apart by false teachers? Of course he won't. And the best way he knows of guarding the truth is to teach it. So the best way he knows of telling the Ephesian shepherds to guard themselves and their flock is to teach the truth over and again.

So, in fear and trembling, we have to say that we, too, are in danger of the wolves and the false shepherds. Calvin says in his commentary on these verses that 'it is the perpetual fate of the church to be infested by wolves'. What is the best way of protecting ourselves; of guarding ourselves?

By teaching, declaring and testifying to the whole counsel of God. That's the job of the church leaders. My job description is *not* to plan great building projects, or visit sick people, or open church fêtes, or a thousand other things I could do. Many of them I should do, and so should you, because we are Christians. Just because I am a pastor doesn't let me off being a Christian. But my task *as a pastor* is to be a teacher, a preacher, a testifier to the truth.

So please don't get bored with Christian teaching. Blame us when we are dull, or irrelevant, or difficult to understand, or not speaking to real-life issues, but please don't ever think, 'We have a good Bible

164 | THE WORD OF HIS GRACE

teaching ministry here – we are safe from wolves now.' Because that's what the wolves want you to think. You are never safe from wolves. That is why a church's small groups, and children's groups, and nurture groups, and preaching must always study the Bible: because the moment I teach something that isn't in the Bible, I too become a wolf. And those of you who teach in the small groups, or the children's groups, or wherever: you need to take this to heart too. You, like me, are a potential wolf. The safety lies in continuing to teach one another. Shall we agree to do that?

Part IV: Living Acts

17 | Living Acts

This book has been about how we can learn to preach from the book of Acts, and there have been two issues to explore. First has been the question of how the content of Acts becomes the content of a sermon today; second has been ensuring that the sermons in Acts are preached today. It might look as if Acts is a preacher's book – which it is! But it is far more than that, and in this last section it is time to look beyond the sermon or Bible study into the impact that Acts should have on the life of a Christian today. It has been well said that the goal of teaching is not *inf*ormation but *trans*formation, and any sermon that stops short of changing people has failed.

That should be developed further. It is easy to see that an evangelistic sermon ought to change people's lives, and that one that does not aim to do that has failed from the outset. But that is aiming at individual, saving transformation, and it is fairly clear that Acts has more than that alone in its view. It has a pattern of healthy church life, individual and corporate, and the preacher should have that in mind too. Just as each individual – Christian and non-Christian – is called to repent and believe the gospel on a daily basis, so the congregation is challenged in its life together, and much of Luke's material is aimed at corporate repentance and faith: application to the local church.

In this final section I want to suggest eight areas where the book of Acts, if brought home with force, would make a significant impact on any congregation, including those who teach it. This first point is of such critical importance because of a widespread misreading of Acts that it will be dealt with at greater length than the others.

The gospel

Luke has often been criticized for having a rather shallow view of the gospel, at least in Acts. Where, it is asked, is the great understanding of the cross or resurrection that we would expect? The cross is hardly mentioned at all, and the resurrection, when Paul is in Athens for instance, appears as a mere footnote to the sermon. It is an obvious criticism, but rather a quick one; a more careful and patient reading of Acts gives a different complexion to the matter.[1]

To take the matter of the cross first, Luke is clear throughout that the death of Jesus is the only means by which men and women may be forgiven. On Pentecost Sunday, for instance, Jesus' death is mentioned twice (2:23, 36), and it is the necessary precursor to Jesus' resurrection status as the enthroned and eternal King (2:31–33) by whom men and women must be forgiven (2:38). Although he does not spell out the mechanics of this in the way we might expect from, say, Paul, he is still crystal clear. The next sermon, in Acts 3, explicitly ties both the particular man's healing and a generalized offer of forgiveness to the cross: 'But this is how God fulfilled what he had foretold through all the prophets, saying that his Christ would suffer. Repent, then, and turn to God, so that your sins may be wiped out, that times of refreshing may come from the Lord' (3:18–19). The third sermon, in Acts 4, makes exactly the same connections:

---

1. Undergirding the whole matter is that this is volume 2 of Luke's work. Presumably he expects his readers to be familiar with what he has already developed more fully.

It is by the name of Jesus Christ of Nazareth, whom you crucified but whom
God raised from the dead, that this man stands before you healed. He is

'the stone you builders rejected,
  which has become the capstone.'

Salvation is found in no-one else, for there is no other name under heaven
given to men by which we must be saved.

(4:10–12)

Remembering how Luke orders and abbreviates his material on
successive occasions, it would be wrong to expect him to report this
on every occasion. Nevertheless, he does so significantly often that it
is clear that the cross and forgiveness are inextricably tied. As Paul
explained in Pisidian Antioch:

Brothers, children of Abraham, and you God-fearing Gentiles, it is to us that
this message of salvation has been sent. The people of Jerusalem and their
rulers did not recognise Jesus, yet in condemning him they fulfilled the words
of the prophets that are read every Sabbath. Though they found no proper
ground for a death sentence, they asked Pilate to have him executed. When
they had carried out all that was written about him, they took him down
from the tree and laid him in a tomb. But God raised him from the dead, and
for many days he was seen by those who had travelled with him from Galilee
to Jerusalem. They are now his witnesses to our people.

We tell you the good news: what God promised our fathers he has
fulfilled for us, their children, by raising up Jesus. As it is written in the
second Psalm:

'You are my Son;
  today I have become your Father.'

The fact that God raised him from the dead, never to decay, is stated in these
words: 'I will give you the holy and sure blessings promised to David.' So it is
stated elsewhere: 'You will not let your Holy One see decay.' For when David
had served God's purpose in his own generation, he fell asleep; he was buried
with his fathers and his body decayed. But the one whom God raised from
the dead did not see decay.

Therefore, my brothers, I want you to know that through Jesus the
forgiveness of sins is proclaimed to you. Through him everyone who believes

is justified from everything you could not be justified from by the law of
Moses.
(13:26–39)

Jesus' death on the tree

That sermon is one of three linked occasions where it is justified to
say that Luke is explaining how the cross achieves the forgiveness
that God has planned.

- 'The God of our fathers raised Jesus from the dead – whom you
  had killed by hanging him on a tree' (5:30) – Peter and the apostles
  speaking to the council and senate of Jerusalem.
- 'We are witnesses of everything he did in the country of the Jews
  and in Jerusalem. They killed him by hanging him on a tree' (10:39) –
  Peter explaining the gospel to Cornelius.
- 'When they had carried out all that was written about him, they
  took him down from the tree and laid him in a tomb' (13:29) – Paul
  preaching the gospel in Pisidian Antioch.

Those three obviously share the critical description of the cross as
a 'tree', and there is general agreement that the background must lie
in the Old Testament, and specifically in Deuteronomy 21:22–23:

> If a man guilty of a capital offence is put to death and his body is hung on a
> tree, you must not leave his body on the tree overnight. Be sure to bury him
> that same day, because anyone who is hung on a tree is under God's curse. You
> must not desecrate the land the Lord your God is giving you as an inheritance.

In Luke's presentation of the cross, then, the means to forgiveness is
that Jesus himself became a person who was cursed by God.

Jesus' death as the Servant

How the cross becomes that means is made clear by a second set of
explanations, this time to do with Jesus' titles. Speaking to the crowd
after the healing of the lame man, Peter said:

> The God of Abraham, Isaac and Jacob, the God of our fathers, has glorified
> his servant Jesus. You handed him over to be killed, and you disowned him

before Pilate, though he had decided to let him go . . . When God raised up his servant, he sent him first to you to bless you by turning each of you from your wicked ways.

(3:13, 26)

Both his introduction and his conclusion stress Jesus' rôle as God's *servant*. Similarly, when the church was praying after that event, its members asked:

> Indeed Herod and Pontius Pilate met together with the Gentiles and the people of Israel in this city to conspire against your holy servant Jesus, whom you anointed. They did what your power and will had decided beforehand should happen. Now, Lord, consider their threats and enable your servants to speak your word with great boldness. Stretch out your hand to heal and perform miraculous signs and wonders through the name of your holy servant Jesus.
>
> (4:27–30)

Not only is Jesus entitled the 'servant'; in the prayer he is twice entitled God's 'holy servant'.

The prime candidate for the origin of that title has to be the material in Isaiah, the so-called 'Servant Songs'.

- *Isaiah 42:1–4*. The servant is the chosen one in whom God delights, and on whom he places his Spirit. He will bring justice to all nations on the earth by establishing his new law. His rule will be gentle but definite, and globally attractive.
- *Isaiah 49:1–6*. The servant will speak and work to gather the scattered tribes of Israel and Judah and – because that is too small for such a wonderful servant – to be a light to the Gentiles. He will bring salvation to the ends of the earth. In this song there is a slight ambiguity. In verse 3 it appears that Israel is the servant, but in verse 5 the servant has a role towards Israel. Clearly he is part of the people, and to some extent a representative of them, but he cannot be completely identified with the people like a national symbol, for he does things for and to them that they cannot do for and to themselves.
- *Isaiah 50:4–9*. The servant is one who accurately hears from God and

relays that message to others. His work involves him in acute suffering, but despite that shame he stands firm, and ultimately God vindicates him.

- *Isaiah 52:13 – 53:12.* The servant is a man of sorrows, yet vindicated by God in the face of all the nations. He does what Israel cannot do, by bearing her sins for her and being punished in her place. In doing this he dies; yet there is a vindication beyond death in which the forgiveness he has won, and the intercession he therefore makes for sinners, is applied to many, many people.

It is quite hard not to see those passages being the defining content in the title 'Servant'; if so, it clearly explains that the way the death of Jesus achieves salvation for us is by his bearing the punishment our sins deserve. In Isaiah's words:

> it was the Lord's will to crush him and cause him to suffer,
>   and though the Lord makes his life a guilt offering,
> he will see his offspring and prolong his days,
>   and the will of the LORD will prosper in his hand.
> After the suffering of his soul,
>   he will see the light of life and be satisfied;
> by his knowledge my righteous servant will justify many,
>   and he will bear their iniquities.
> Therefore I will give him a portion among the great,
>   and he will divide the spoils with the strong,
> because he poured out his life unto death,
>   and was numbered with the transgressors.
> For he bore the sin of many,
>   and made intercession for the transgressors.
> (Isa. 53:10–12)

Or, as Peter put it:

> The God of Abraham, Isaac and Jacob, the God of our fathers, has glorified his servant Jesus. You handed him over to be killed, and you disowned him before Pilate, though he had decided to let him go. You disowned the Holy and Righteous One and asked that a murderer be released to you. You killed the author of life, but God raised him from the dead. We are witnesses of this . . .

But this is how God fulfilled what he had foretold through all the prophets, saying that his Christ would suffer. Repent, then, and turn to God, so that your sins may be wiped out, that times of refreshing may come from the Lord.
(Acts 3:3–15, 18–19)

Critically, at the moment when Philip explains the gospel to the Ethiopian, the latter has been reading from that final servant song (8:32–33).

Jesus' resurrection as vindication
As each of the sermons in Acts has been looked at, it has become clear that Jesus' resurrection was no mere afterthought by God, and that Luke has a coherent theology of why he was raised from the dead. Four observations are in order.

Jesus' resurrection and vindication is implicit in the Old Testament prophecies.
There are two Old Testament prophecies quoted in Acts which demonstrate a pattern that the coming Messiah/King/Servant would suffer, and then after suffering to the point of death would be vindicated by God and established in a pre-eminent position.

> I saw the Lord always before me
>> Because he is at my right hand,
>> I will not be shaken.
> Therefore my heart is glad and my tongue rejoices;
>> my body also will live in hope,
> because you will not abandon me to the grave,
>> nor will you let your Holy One see decay.
> You have made known to me the paths of life;
>> you will fill me with joy in your presence.
> (Acts 2:25–28. quoting Ps. 16:8–11)

> The stone the builders rejected
>> has become the capstone;
> the LORD has done this,
>> and it is marvellous in our eyes.
> (Ps. 118:22–23, quoted in Acts 4:11)

Two others accompany those in their context, indicating the honour that was expected to be given to this vindicated King.

> The LORD said to my Lord:
> 'Sit at my right hand
> until I make your enemies
> a footstool for your feet.'
> (Acts 2:34, quoting Ps. 110:1)

> Why do the nations rage
> and the peoples plot in vain?
> The kings of the earth take their stand
> and the rulers gather together
> against the Lord
> and against his Anointed One.
> (Acts 4:25–26, quoting Ps. 2:1–2)

This suffering and vindication motif had already been indicated by Luke as a critical way of understanding the death of Jesus. After his resurrection, Jesus met two of his disciples and said:

> 'How foolish you are, and how slow of heart to believe all that the prophets have spoken! Did not the Christ have to suffer these things and then enter his glory?' And beginning with Moses and all the Prophets, he explained to them what was said in all the Scriptures concerning himself.
> (Luke 24:25–27)

Later, he explained to them all:

> 'This is what I told you while I was still with you: everything must be fulfilled that is written about me in the Law of Moses, the Prophets and the Psalms.' Then he opened their minds so they could understand the Scriptures. He told them, 'This is what is written: the Christ will suffer and rise from the dead on the third day, and repentance and forgiveness of sins will be preached in his name to all nations, beginning at Jerusalem. You are witnesses of these things.'
> (Luke 24:44–48)

Jesus' resurrection and vindication are public statements by God
Jesus' initial authorization of the apostles introduced a term which we
have already noted as significant: witness. 'But you will receive power
when the Holy Spirit comes on you; and you will be my *witnesses* in
Jerusalem, and in all Judea and Samaria, and to the ends of the earth'
(1:8). Each time Luke uses it of the apostles, it is with the precise sense
of someone who needs to be able to give a public testimony of God's
action in raising Jesus from the dead. It is a legal concept.

> Therefore it is necessary to choose one of the men who have been with us
> the whole time the Lord Jesus went in and out among us, beginning from
> John's baptism to the time when Jesus was taken up from us. For one of
> these must become a *witness* with us of his resurrection.
>
> (1:21–22)

> God has raised this Jesus to life, and we are all *witnesses* of the fact.
>
> (2:32)

> You killed the author of life, but God raised him from the dead. We are
> *witnesses* of this.
>
> (3:15)

> God exalted him to his own right hand as Prince and Saviour that he might
> give repentance and forgiveness of sins to Israel. We are *witnesses* of these
> things, and so is the Holy Spirit, whom God has given to those who obey him.
>
> (5:31–32)

> We are *witnesses* of everything he did in the country of the Jews and in
> Jerusalem. They killed him by hanging him on a tree, but God raised him
> from the dead on the third day and caused him to be seen. He was not seen
> by all the people, but by *witnesses* whom God had already chosen – by us
> who ate and drank with him after he rose from the dead. He commanded us
> to preach to the people and to testify that he is the one whom God appointed
> as judge of the living and the dead.
>
> (10:39–42)

> But God raised him from the dead, and for many days he was seen by those
> who had travelled with him from Galilee to Jerusalem. They are now his
> *witnesses* to our people.
>
> (13:30–31)

In two accounts of Paul's conversion and commissioning as an apostle, which included a resurrection appearance from heaven:

> You will be his *witness* to all men of what you have seen and heard.
> (22:15)

> Now get up and stand on your feet. I have appeared to you to appoint you as a servant and as a *witness* of what you have seen of me and what I will show you.
> (26:16)

This gives the early church the basis of its message, and also its authority to speak. Peter explained this connection most clearly in his conversation with Cornelius, when he said:

> [Jesus] was not seen by all the people, but by *witnesses* whom God had already chosen – by us who ate and drank with him after he rose from the dead. He commanded us to preach to the people and to testify that he is the one whom God appointed as judge of the living and the dead.
> (Acts 10:41–42)

The resurrection is therefore something that the church has a duty to proclaim, and that the world has a right – and need – to hear about.

Jesus' resurrection and vindication are the basis for his present ministry from heaven

Jesus' resurrection and ascension do not remove him from earthly concerns. Rather, the defining centre of world history is relocated to his throne, and everything else is to be understood as under his reign from there. His place there is established frequently in Acts (1:2, 11; 2:34; 3:21; 7:55–56; 9:3ff; 22:6ff; 26:13ff), and it is from there that he dispenses his good gifts. It is precisely because he is enthroned that he is in a position to pour out the Spirit and to offer forgiveness in his name, as Peter argued in chapter 2. And it is precisely because he is located outside the land that the gospel can freely move there, as Stephen argued in chapter 7. His speech ended with his triumphant shout, 'Look, . . . I see heaven open and the Son of Man standing at the right hand of God' (7:56). Hence a physical resurrection, seen by 'witnesses . . . who ate and drank with him after he rose from the dead' (10:41), is followed by a physical ascension and a real and ongoing ministry by a living Lord Jesus. Jesus' current ministry is the application of the benefits won by his death. Nor is that the end; for 'This same Jesus, who has been taken from you into heaven, will come back in the same way you have seen him go into heaven' (1:11).

Jesus' resurrection and vindication are the proof of the existence of Judgment Day, and therefore of his role as Judge and Saviour on that Day

From the outset of Acts, then, Jesus' physical return to heaven functions as an enthronement. If we combine the various elements of the Old Testament background that this section has covered, it becomes apparent that this post-death enthronement must involve him in judgment and victory over his enemies, even as he saves his people whose punishment he has already borne. Psalm 110, which Peter quoted at Pentecost to establish that this pattern is thoroughly rooted in the Old Testament, talks of 'the day of [God's] wrath' (Ps. 110:5). God's appointed and anointed King was expected to act in final judgment and victory.

All of this cumulative thinking lies behind what Paul was explaining in Athens. The initial puzzlement is caused by his 'preaching the good news about Jesus and the resurrection' (17:18), and he later explains the connection between those two in terms that should be familiar to Luke's readers. God 'has set a day when he will judge the world with justice by the man he has appointed. He has given proof of this to all men by raising him from the dead' (17:31). Far from being a truncated gospel, the message that Paul gives, and which Luke has presumably distilled, is one that encompasses the broad sweep of biblical theology at its most central and focuses on the role of Jesus in a most critical way.

Once readers have become attuned to Luke's way of explaining Paul's theology, it is apparent that his thinking is no thinner or less thought-through than that expressed in the letters; nor does it leave the gospels behind. It simply explains things differently. Rather than explain the working of the cross, he uses Jesus' titles (such as Servant or Judge) and a wealth of interlocking Old Testament material to do the work for him. But there is no doubt that he understood that

Jesus' death was as our sin-bearing, judgment-bearing, punishment-bearing, wrath-appeasing substitute.

Evangelism

If all that is true, then the content for our evangelism – the message to spread – is clear and unchanging. While we are not the direct witnesses, the command to tell the world what the witnesses saw and the command to repent and believe in the light of the coming Day of Judgment cannot be evaded. One direct consequence of an encounter with Acts must be that our evangelistic passion is reignited, and it must be reignited with this precise gospel. Any other message is not the authentic message of New Testament Christianity, and that means it will not save its hearers.

So our imagination is reignited too. More than once, Acts has shown us the flexibility and creativity of the early church as it sought to win its world. So too today, then, we need to be questioning our methods and language all the time, to see if they are effectively reaching non-Christians with this unchanging message. It is common for the church to have internal debates about doctrine, and that is a right concern. It is much rarer to find churches fired up to reach out with the message and willing to pay the high prices which that requires.

Church planting

It is nearly eighty years since the great missionary thinker Roland Allen first published his two groundbreaking books, *Missionary Methods: St Paul's or Ours* and *The Spontaneous Expansion of the Church and the Causes which Hinder it*.[2] Reflecting on his time in China from 1895 to 1903, he challenged many of the principles of mission agencies in his day and argued that there is in Paul's ministry a pattern

---

2. *Missionary Methods* (first published in 1912) and *Spontaneous Expansion* (first published in 1927) have both been reprinted many times, currently by Eerdmans (Grand Rapids, 1962).

which God intended the church permanently to adopt, of church planting. He argued that although it looks as if Paul deliberately selected particular cities to work in as being the key to an area or province, the movement was not the result of careful planning and strategy, but rather of faithful preaching and spontaneous response to the work of the Spirit.

The books themselves are thrilling to read, and, even if some of his findings have been more carefully nuanced, it does seem clear that Luke is commending what he did, summarized as 'the work' (13:2, 14:26, 15:38). David Hesselgrave has argued that Paul was more systematic than Allen suggests, following the steps of contacting the audience, communicating the gospel, converting the hearers, forming a congregation, strengthening the believers, appointing leaders and continuing their nurture.[3] That is certainly plausible from Acts, and means that we have both a mandate and a model to follow here. That is, not only would reading Acts leave a church wanting to plant a congregation; it would provide the essential elements of a strategy.

Discipling

It was noted above in passing how Acts 14:21–22 functions as a little summary of how Christian evangelism and discipling go together.

> Paul and Barnabas preached the good news in Derbe and won a large number of disciples. Then they returned to Lystra, Iconium and Antioch, strengthening the disciples and encouraging them to remain true to the faith. 'We must go through many hardships to enter the kingdom of God,' they said.

In a convenient nutshell Luke has demonstrated that the evangelism which bore fruit was not allowed to flourish on its own, but that the

---

3. David Hesselgrave, *Planting Churches Cross-Culturally: A Guide for Home and Foreign Missions* (Grand Rapids: Baker, 1992). His sequence of planting is fuller than I have suggested here.

workers nourished it, and the diet they fed the fledgling church was one of standing firm under suffering. In some parts of the world this is so obvious it hardly bears comment, but this is such an unusual feature, at least to the eyes of a Christian from the West, that it bears careful thought. Perhaps a number of our discipleship programmes would be substantially more biblical, and therefore substantially more effective, if they included the cost of Christian discipleship from the outset, and therefore the inevitability of cultural opposition to the Christian lifestyle.

That discipling would also include a second feature of the early church which is easily missed, which is their attitude to finances. Three occasions in the narrative are worth noting.

The Jerusalem church

From the outset Luke notes that 'All the believers were together and had everything in common. Selling their possessions and goods, they gave to anyone as he had need' (2:44–45). That is in a section which is clearly identifiable as an ideal for other churches to copy, even though it has elements which are unique and unrepeatable. There is a clearer spotlight placed on the issue shortly afterwards, when Luke is scene setting.

> All the believers were one in heart and mind. No-one claimed that any of his possessions was his own, but they shared everything they had. With great power the apostles continued to testify to the resurrection of the Lord Jesus, and much grace was upon them all. There were no needy persons among them. For from time to time those who owned lands or houses sold them, brought the money from the sales and put it at the apostles' feet, and it was distributed to anyone as he had need.
>
> (4:32–35)

That general and attractive picture is exemplified in Barnabas, who 'sold a field he owned and brought the money and put it at the apostles' feet' (v. 37), and is in dramatic contrast to Ananias, who 'also sold a piece of property. With his wife's full knowledge he kept back part of the money for himself, but brought the rest and put it at the apostles' feet' (5:1–2). The key issue is the lie that Ananias was telling with this action, and Peter exposed that he had lied to the Holy Spirit in keeping for himself some of the money he received for the land.

Didn't it belong to you before it was sold? And after it was sold, wasn't the money at your disposal? (5:3–4). Handing over all the money was not compulsory, but generosity and honesty were. Discipleship, then, was demonstrable in the use that people made of their money and property.

The famine collection

The second noteworthy occasion was when Paul (still called Saul at this stage) and Barnabas were in Antioch.

> [F]or a whole year Barnabas and Saul met with the church and taught great numbers of people. The disciples were called Christians first at Antioch.
>
> During this time some prophets came down from Jerusalem to Antioch. One of them, named Agabus, stood up and through the Spirit predicted that a severe famine would spread over the entire Roman world. (This happened during the reign of Claudius.) The disciples, each according to his ability, decided to provide help for the brothers living in Judea. This they did, sending their gift to the elders by Barnabas and Saul.
>
> (11:26–30)

At this significant moment the direction of travel reversed, and the Antioch church, the centre of the Gentile mission, becomes the benefactor of the Jerusalem congregation. It is striking to note both the immediacy and the seriousness of the collection; this seems to have been the beginnings of the collection that Paul organized and which cost him personally so much.[4] Loyalty to and love for suffering sisters and brothers was expressed in financial terms.

The Ephesian elders

The third occasion to notice occurs at the climax of Paul's speech to the Ephesian elders at Miletus. After all the terrible and necessary warnings about the nature of Christian leadership, Paul concludes:

> I have not coveted anyone's silver or gold or clothing. You yourselves know that these hands of mine have supplied my own needs and the needs of my

---

4. Gal. 2:10; 1 Cor. 16:1–4; 2 Cor. 8 – 9.

companions. In everything I did, I showed you that by this kind of hard work we must help the weak, remembering the words the Lord Jesus himself said: 'It is more blessed to give than to receive.'

(20:33–35)

That concluding moment, quoting words of Jesus we would not otherwise have recorded, is surely meant to be as critical and programmatic for the life of the church as all the preceding material. Leaders are supposed to demonstrate their discipleship by their attitude to money, which is to be observable and generous.

Producing resources on discipleship which leave suffering unaddressed is not preparing Christians adequately for the world around, even if Western Christians find that hard to believe. But Western Christians might find resources which make financial generosity a basic mark of discipleship much harder to obey, and that might be precisely because we can see its immediate relevance and perhaps, like Ananias, wish to pretend to be more generous than we actually are.

Suffering

We have already noted the fact that preparation for suffering seems to have been a standard element in basic Christian nurture. We must not become lopsided on this, of course, because the story of the book of Acts is of wonderful gospel growth, church planting and evangelistic endeavour. But it does seem that the two are connected, even though that may not seem to be common sense.

Take as an example Paul's ministry, which is useful because we have an expanded presentation of it and because, while there are elements which are clearly Apostolic, there are others which are transferable. God prepared Ananias to meet the new convert, and said, 'This man is my chosen instrument to carry my name before the Gentiles and their kings and before the people of Israel. I will show him how much he must suffer for my name' (9:15–16). It is that very carrying of the message which produces the suffering. Later, Paul assures those same Ephesian elders that:

[C]ompelled by the Spirit, I am going to Jerusalem, not knowing what will happen to me there. I only know that in every city the Holy Spirit warns me that prison and hardships are facing me. However, I consider my life worth nothing to me, if only I may finish the race and complete the task the Lord Jesus has given me – the task of testifying to the gospel of God's grace. (20:22–24).[5]

And Agabus prophesied quite accurately that 'The Holy Spirit says, "In this way the Jews of Jerusalem will bind the owner of this belt and will hand him over to the Gentiles"' (21:11). Paul's destiny was to imitate the suffering of his master and show the intimately painful nature of Christian ministry.

Once again, the Western church often seems too occupied with success or growth to notice that these are not alternatives to suffering and persecution, but their twins. Of course one can think of churches which have seen unbroken success, for which everyone praises God, and churches which have seen suffering that has produced nothing, or even faithlessness. But normally the two sides of the equation balance: a church which is faithful to God will at some stage experience suffering for that faithfulness, and a church which is suffering is nurtured to a deeper discipleship by her loving Lord.

Prayer

It was in response to several of these elements, and not least to suffering, that the early church learned the lessons of vital and confident praying to God. An obvious instance is the response to the initial opposition by the Jerusalem authorities in chapter 4:23–31. They will not be stopped in their proclamation by this political ban; they pray for confidence and for God to act miraculously both in their defence and in winning people to him. Their confidence is, once again, set up by Luke as a model.

---

5. The phrase 'finish the race' is obviously reminiscent of 2 Tim. 4:7. For further thought on this, see my *Finishing the Race: Preaching 2 Timothy Today* (Sydney: Aquila, 2000).

In case we are tempted to fantasize about these Christians, though, it is worth remembering their reaction to Peter's imprisonment in chapter 12. They had seen James arrested and executed, so we can imagine their reaction to hearing the news about their other leader. As we would expect, and as we would hope about ourselves, 'Peter was kept in prison, but the church was earnestly praying to God for him' (12:5). They kept on praying hard, too, because once Peter was miraculously released (which was presumably one outcome they were praying for) he went 'to the house of Mary the mother of John, also called Mark, where many people had gathered and were praying' (12:12). So far the story is smooth. But the wrinkle comes when Peter knocked at the door, as the answer to their payers, and they refused to believe that their prayers have been answered and ignored him – presumably to carry on praying for Peter's release.

So there is no place to romanticize these Christians, who were, Luke seems deliberately to be telling us, just ordinary Christians. Nevertheless, that description may be too flattering, if we think of ourselves equally as ordinary Christians. Luke may be telling his story in an almost humorous way as he recounts their all-night prayer vigil, but at least they had one. Equally, the appointment of Paul and Barnabas occurred at a prayer meeting.

> While they were worshipping the Lord and fasting, the Holy Spirit said, 'Set apart for me Barnabas and Saul for the work to which I have called them.' So after they had fasted and prayed, they placed their hands on them and sent them off. The two of them, sent on their way by the Holy Spirit, went down to Seleucia and sailed from there to Cyprus.
>
> (13:2–4)

The activity of the Spirit is obviously related in that section to their praying; it is presumably also indicated in the move to mainland Europe (16:6–10). We noted previously that the presence of signs and/or wonders is limited to the first half of Acts, before the Council of Jerusalem, and is not evenly spread through the book. That is no doubt because Luke is explaining Peter's use of the Joel prophecy, especially 2:18–19. But even if we strip out from Acts the elements which were unique to the ministry of the apostles precisely because they were apostles, and those elements which are unique to the age when the risen Lord Jesus was authenticating his witnesses, we are still left with a series of congregations which were spiritually alert, in both their praying and their expectation of God's activity. They form a striking, and sobering, contrast to many churches today.

Preaching

It is too simple to say that Acts is about church growth, and Luke's little summary verses will not allow that to stand. Repeatedly the activity of the church is described as preaching or teaching 'the word',[6] but on several occasions something even more striking happened. 'So the word of God spread' (6:7); 'But the word of God continued to increase and spread' (12:24); 'The word of the Lord spread through the whole region' (13:49); 'In this way the word of the Lord spread widely and grew in power' (19:20). As more than one writer has suggested, the real hero of the book of Acts is the word of God.

Since our culture is notoriously anti-word, and since that inevitably infects the church, it is perhaps worth observing one last time how Paul conducts his ministry. In Thessalonica, 'As his custom was, Paul went into the synagogue, and on three Sabbath days he reasoned with them from the Scriptures, explaining and proving that the Christ had to suffer and rise from the dead. "This Jesus I am proclaiming to you is the Christ," he said' (17:2–3). The response was that people were 'persuaded' (17:4). After leading Bible studies in Berea (17:10–12) and teaching the resurrection in Athens (17:16–34), Paul arrived in Corinth, where again 'Every Sabbath he reasoned in the synagogue, trying to persuade Jews and Greeks' and 'devoted himself exclusively to preaching, testifying to the Jews that Jesus was the Christ' (Acts 18:4–5). That attention to careful, explanatory, Bible-based teaching, preaching and evangelism is not fashionable and appears unwise. But if all the other items on the list in this section are the way the early church is designed to serve as a template and

---

6. 4:29, 31; 6:2, 4; 8:4, 14, 25; 11:1; 13:5, 7, 44, 46, 48; 14:25; 15:35, 36; 16:6, 32; 17:13; 18:11; 19:10; 20:32.

corrective to our culture-bound weaknesses, then here, too, we shall have to change. That, of course, ensures God is sovereign, for only he controls the response. In Pisidian Antioch 'When the Gentiles heard this, they were glad and honoured the word of the Lord; and all who were appointed for eternal life believed' (13:48), and in Philippi 'One of those listening was a woman named Lydia, a dealer in purple cloth from the city of Thyatira, who was a worshipper of God. The Lord opened her heart to respond to Paul's message' (16:14). The open Bible is God's way to change lives in Acts.

Leadership

One final set of observations should be made which present a challenge to the church today from Acts. Parallel to the argument that Paul had a strategy for planting churches is an argument that he had a strategy for nurturing the next generation of leaders. It is possible to be too prescriptive here, but it is worth considering the training of Timothy, who is presented at least to some extent as a working example.

A	16:1–2	As a mature, if young, believer, he is nominated by the church to Paul and accepted by him as a travelling companion, along with Silas.
B	17:14–15	Timothy, partnered by Silas, is left in Berea to look after the new church; Paul sails for Athens.
C	18:5	They rejoin Paul, who has since moved on to Corinth.
D	19:22	Timothy is sent with Erastus to Macedonia to pioneer new work ahead of Paul.
E	20:1–4	Paul travels through Macedonia, where (presumably) he and Timothy meet.

Table 17.1

Although the story told through the passages listed in Table 17.1 is sketchy, it is very tempting to see a pattern where Paul (A) takes on a young man; (B) leaves him with some responsibility and a mentor; (C) recalls him; (D) leaves him with a greater responsibility and a younger leader to mentor; and (E) meets them again.

There a number of other co-workers of Paul listed in Acts.

- *Barnabas*, who began as a Jerusalem delegate to Antioch (11:22–24); became Paul's own mentor (11:25); discipled him as his equal (11:26); and, even though they separated, remained a fellow worker in the gospel.
- *John Mark*, whom Paul and Barnabas jointly mentored (12:25) and who remained loyal to Barnabas in the dispute and followed him to Cyprus (15:35–39), but who finished as helpful to Paul in ministry (2 Tim. 4:11).
- *Priscilla and Aquila*, who in Acts meet Paul (18:2); spend time with him (18:18); are left to work (18:19); and engage in discipling Apollos, among others (18:26).
- *A whole crowd* of others, including Gaius and Aristarchus (19:29); Sopater son of Pyrrhus from Berea; Secundus from Thessalonica; and Tychicus and Trophimus from the province of Asia (20:4).
- And, presumably, *Luke* himself, in the 'we' parts of the narrative.

And, to show the pattern developing further,

- *Apollos*, who had been treated by Priscilla and Aquila in the way Paul had treated them, went to evangelize in Achaia (18:27–28).

Even from within the text of Acts, then, there is clear evidence that Paul not only saw himself as a member of a team, but took the responsibility of nurturing the next generation, through teaching, exposure, responsibility and accountability.[7]

Churches, then, should take this responsibility seriously, and not assume that the next generation of pastors will appear without any work on their part. God was clearly at work in these selections, but so too were human wisdom, decision-making and, on one occasion,

---

7. This pattern is clearly expanded in the letters. See, for instance, F. F. Bruce, *The Pauline Circle* (London: Paternoster, 1985).

a cooling-off period to allow growth. Perhaps alongside the renewed passion for evangelism, discipling, church planting, prayer and preaching which Acts has put before us, a renewed passion for the next generation of leaders should be in place.

Conclusion

Reading, studying and preaching from Acts is an exhilarating experience, but living it out, or attempting to live it out, as a church member or leader is a humbling one too. The comparisons are designed to stretch us and make us want to grow, but they also serve to keep us in our place and recall that it is the Lord Jesus, and not us, who is on the throne.

Acts is also designed to equip us, though, and that is a confidence which we would do well to recover. Paul told the Ephesian elders: 'Now I commit you to God and to the word of his grace, which can build you up and give you an inheritance among all those who are sanctified' (20:32), which implies that what he taught them was adequate to equip them for the task. If that same word of grace has been carefully thought through by Luke and recorded here for our benefit, then the book of Acts will build us up too, and give us the inheritance God has promised to all his saints.

We began by noting that commentaries on books tend to be longer than the books they are commenting on, and that Acts is, after Luke's Gospel, the longest work in the New Testament. This book was intended to be brief and to function as an overview, but the serious preacher will need to read further. For a full survey of commentaries, consult the *New Testament Commentary Survey* by **D. A. Carson** (Grand Rapids MI: Baker/Leicester: Inter-Varsity Press, 5th edn, 2001), which is both exhaustive and judicious.

There are a number of commentaries which should help the preacher with the next stage of understanding the text, among which are **William J. Larkin**, *Acts* (IVP New Testament Commentary series, Downers Grove, IL/Leicester: Inter-Varsity Press, 1995) and **David J. Williams**, *Acts* (New International Biblical Commentary, Peabody, MA/Paternoster Press, Carlisle Hendrickson: 1999). They are both clear and thought-provoking, and Larkin opens his commentary with a section on preaching, which shows where his heart lies. **John Stott** has contributed the Bible Speaks Today volume (Leicester: Inter-Varsity Press, 1990), which is particularly strong in demonstrating how Acts can be communicated with clarity. **David Gooding** has written *True to the Faith: Charting the Course through the Acts of the Apostles* (Port Colborne, ON: Gospel Folio Press, 2001), which, as the subtitle indicates, has a stress on the structural issues in Acts. **I. H. Marshall** has contributed the Tyndale commentary (Leicester: Inter-Varsity Press, 1980), which is more thorough than any of those others, although it now looks a little dated because of the way Acts studies have moved on, in a largely positive direction. Much older, but for that very reason surprisingly fresh, is the work of **John Calvin**, available in various editions. In my judgment the single commentary which best accomplishes all these various tasks is by **Richard N. Longenecker** in the Expositor's Bible Commentary, volume 8 (Grand Rapids: Zondervan, 1991).

More technical and textually oriented commentaries include two recent revisions of the substantial commentaries by **F. F. Bruce**: one on the English text, *The Book of the Acts* (New International Commentary on the New Testament, Grand Rapids: Eerdmans, 1998), and one on the Greek, *The Acts of the Apostles* (Grand Rapids: Eerdmans, 1990). **C. K. Barrett** has produced the two volumes of the International Critical Commentary (Edinburgh: T. & T. Clark, vol. 1, 1994, vol. 2, 1998). With such attention to critical detail and essential close reading, there is a constant tendency to lose the architecture of the book, but Bruce on the English is the best of this pack.

Three trends in New Testament scholarship which usually complement each other, but occasionally contradict, have contributed to a new wave of fresh thinking about Acts. The first is an increasing awareness of the historical authenticity of Acts, and the crowning glory of that is a five-volume series, *The Book of Acts in its First Century Setting* (Grand Rapids: Eerdmans/Carlisle: Paternoster, various dates), with **Bruce Winter** acting as the series editor. Each volume looks at a different aspect of that setting, whether literary or socio-political. A final volume of essays addressing theological issues was published as *Witness to the Word* (eds. I. H. Marshall and D. Peterson, Grand Rapids: Eerdmans/Carlisle: Paternoster, 1998). This series has turned a major corner in Acts studies.

A second trend is the discipline of narrative criticism, which takes Luke seriously as a careful storyteller. More academically rigorous than Gooding (who has also written on Luke's gospel) is **Robert C. Tannehill**'s two-volume, *The Narrative Unity of Luke-Acts: A Literary*

Interpretation (Minneapolis: Fortress Press, 1994), which was a pioneering work and never fails to be sparkling and insightful. This is essential reading. **Luke Timothy Johnson**'s substantial work takes a very similar line, but with more interest in Luke as a *literary historian*, arguing that Luke uses 'fictional shaping' of his material as a legitimate literary tool for any historian, ancient or contemporary (*Sacra Pagina* vol. 5, Collegeville: The Liturgical Press, 1992). Various subsets of this trend have emerged. **Beverly Roberts Gaventa** has written a short and accessible commentary focusing on the theology of Acts (Abingdon New Testament Commentaries, Nashville: Abingdon, 2003). **F. Scott Spencer** pays particular attention to engaging with the insights of cultural anthropologists and social scientists into the codes and systems of the first-century world (*Acts*, Sheffield: Sheffield Academic Press, 1997).

The third discipline is rhetorical criticism, which addresses the issue of the style in which Luke wrote as a first-century historian, and **Ben Witherington III** has written a large 'socio-rhetorical commentary' which has this as a particular focus (Grand Rapids: Eerdmans/Carlisle: Paternoster, 1998).

In my view, then, the best buy for an initial commentary on Acts would be Longenecker, and the best for substantial thought would come with a combination of Bruce and Tannehill. In progress, and worth consulting when they arrive, will be the work of **Paul Barnett**, which will focus on historical issues; the Word Commentary by **Steven Walton**; the New International Commentary on the New Testament by **Joel Green**; and the Pillar New Testament Commentary by **David Peterson**.